BRUNEL AND AFTER

THE ROMANCE OF THE GREAT WESTERN RAILWAY

THE COMPLETION by Patrick Stephens of their successful series of facsimile reprints of the seven books in the GWR's popular "Boys of All Ages" series led to many requests for this reprint of "Brunel and After", first published by the GWR in 1925.

Isambard Kingdom Brunel accomplished countless awe-inspiring feats of engineering during his life and many of these owe their existence to the Great Western Railway, of which he was engineer from its inception in 1833 until his death in 1859. One of his few failures followed his imaginative introduction of the broad gauge and the struggle to retain it provides the climax in Mr Williams' story. Sadly, Brunel was a few years too late, for the standard gauge was already well on the way to establishing itself and the GWR was finally compelled to begin the costly and laborious conversion. However, the great engineer had laid solid foundations for the Great Western, and the book reveals the dignity and courage which this famous railway showed throughout its turbulent career, how it overcame its failures and how it grew to be the greatest in the British Isles.

This story of the Great Western Railway from 1833 to 1924 makes compulsive reading for historians, railway modellers and laymen alike. This new edition is a close facsimile of the original, the only differences being that it is hard bound, has a new introduction and a redesigned jacket, and the gatefold route map has been reproduced in two, not three colours.

I. K. BRUNEL.

ENGINEER OF THE GREAT WESTERN RAILWAY (1833-1858)

BRUNEL AND AFTER

THE ROMANCE OF THE
GREAT WESTERN RAILWAY

BY

ARCHIBALD WILLIAMS

WITH 78 ILLUSTRATIONS

PUBLISHED IN 1925 BY
THE GREAT WESTERN RAILWAY
[FELIX J. C. POLE, GENERAL MANAGER]
PADDINGTON STATION, LONDON

First published 1925
Reprinted 1972

ISBN 0 85059 092 2

385·09423/3

Reproduced by offset lithography from the original
by Compton Printing Ltd, of Aylesbury, England, and
bound by Hunter & Foulis Ltd, of Edinburgh, Scotland,
for the publishers, Patrick Stephens Limited,
9 Ely Place, London EC1N 6SQ, England.

INTRODUCTION TO NEW EDITION

ISAMBARD KINGDOM BRUNEL accomplished many awe-inspiring feats of engineering in the 52 years of his life, and a good number of these famous constructions owe their existence to the Great Western Railway, of which he was engineer from its inception in 1833 until his death in 1859.

Sadly, as this book shows, Brunel's contributions to the Great Western Railway could not be counted as a complete triumph. His imaginative introduction of the broad gauge was doomed from the start and the struggle to retain it provides the climax in Mr. Williams' story as he relates the frantic races against time to prove that this was the speediest and most comfortable medium for rail travel. But it was all in vain for, before the Great Western Railway Act had even been presented to Parliament, the standard gauge had spread its tracks across the British countryside and in 1869 the management of the G.W.R. found itself compelled, for long-term financial and practical reasons, to begin the costly conversion to the 'narrow gauge', as it was then called. However, Brunel had laid solid foundations for the Great Western during his lifetime, and the book reveals the dignity and courage which this famous railway showed throughout its turbulent career, how it overcame its failures and how it grew to be the greatest in the British Isles.

The author includes a useful appendix of some principal dates in Great Western Railway history from 1833 to 1924, when he wrote the book. This list gives at a glance basic information on developments in the railway and is invaluable for those, such as historians and railway modellers, who wish to pinpoint certain events. However, this story of the Great Western Railway makes compulsive reading for the layman, too; tales such as that of the passengers who would rather "disembark" when nearing a long tunnel and walk across the hill to catch a train at the other side than be subjected to the terrors of subterranean travel, conjure up the pre-commuter age when a train journey was a stimulating adventure and the making of a railway the work of a pioneering visionary such as Brunel.

Sue Fletcher

FOREWORD

IT is probably the experience of many people that one particular long railway journey stands out in memory as having been enjoyable above all others. The same journey might be repeated, but without giving the same pleasure, because the full setting of it—which includes not merely the physical surroundings and mechanical means of locomotion—cannot be restaged.

In my own case I have no hesitation in giving first place to a run which I made over the Great Western Railway in 1910 : the last stage of a journey home from Central America. The earlier stages had not been without interest, but travelling for days on end through deserts, prairies and mountains becomes monotonous, and the Atlantic in dull and gusty weather does not improve on acquaintance. How welcome was the little tender that at last came out from Plymouth to land passengers and mails from the great liner : how deliciously *green* the Devon landscape looked after the incessant browns and greys of the last fortnight ! After the custom-house formalities came the settling-down in the luxurious Ocean Mails Special, which soon pulled out of Millbay Station on its non-stop run to Paddington through country glorious with the beauties of a perfect day in early June. First, the grand inland scenery of South Devon ; then the waterside stretch from Newton to Exeter, along a narrow ledge of permanent way ; followed by the ever-changing, if quieter, views of the pastoral counties of Somerset, Wilts and Berkshire, with their old villages and churches and trim-hedged fields, all doubly welcome to the eye of the returned traveller.

A perfect run under conditions ideal for a proper appreciation.

The Great Western Railway has pleasurable associations for many people, for is it not the pathway to the great holiday grounds of the western counties and Wales ? Many books have been written about the resorts and places and scenes of interest to be reached by " going Great Western "; until, indeed, there seems little more to be said. This little volume is intended rather to give, in a handy form, some account of the history of the railway itself.

The subject has to be treated broadly, owing to limitations of space, and anything in the nature of a complete record— which would require more than one bulky tome—is therefore not to be looked for. It is hoped, however, that what is here printed will be of interest not only to the travelling public, but to many of those who are employed in the service of the Great Western Railway.

That the book is entirely free from error, is too much to expect, though an honest endeavour to be accurate has been made. In the matter of dates, for example, it is often diffi- cult to nail down a happening exactly. Even good authori- ties sometimes differ. Any corrections that may be embodied in future editions will be welcomed.

So now for a two-hour run through Great Western Annals from the great days of Brunel and Gooch and Saunders and the broad gauge and the eight-foot " singles " to what may appear the more prosaic times in which the infant of 1838 has reached its full stature as a great system covering not only the West of England and South Wales, but the Cambrian Coast and a large part of the Midlands. May it be a pleasant one for the reader !

CHAPTERS

WITH 78 ILLUSTRATIONS

THE PRELIMINARY STAGES

FOR some centuries Bristol was the second most important town in England. From its port sailed, in 1497, John Cabot on the voyage which ended in the discovery of the mainland of N. America. From Bristol started, in 1838, the first ship to travel from England to New York and back under steam all the way. This vessel, the *Great Western*,* made the outward journey in 15 days, and the homeward journey in 14, effectively rebutting the opinion of the then famous Dr. Lardner, that the extreme limit of a steamer's practicable voyage without refuelling was about 2,000 miles.

During the period between these two important events Bristol became, and continued to be, the leading port of entry of the West of England, thanks to the energy and enterprise of its Merchant Adventurers. The growth of trade rendered more and more important the question of easy communication with the main centres of consumption, notably London.

The main roads of the country were greatly improved during the last quarter of the eighteenth and the first quarter of the nineteenth century, but, as road haulage between Bath and London cost from 5s. to 6s. per

* *See page* 6

1

hundredweight, the transport of heavy merchandise by road was usually out of the question.

In 1810 matters were improved by the opening of the Kennet and Avon Canal, which united a tributary of the Thames with a tributary of the Severn, and so gave Bristol water communication with London by barge. But what with ice and floods in winter, and low water in canal and rivers in summer, the new mode of conveyance left very much to be desired, and eventually conditions became so unbearable that the leading merchants of Bristol began to look to the construction of a railway as the only way out of their troubles.

An abortive attempt to organise a railway company was made as early as 1825, the year of the opening of the Stockton and Darlington line. Several years later, when the Liverpool and Manchester Railway had proved a great success, fresh steps were taken. In May, 1832, appeared a prospectus of a projected " Bristol and London Railway " (observe·the order), in which the cost was estimated at £2,500,000, and the annual net revenue at £360,000 ; and this was followed, a month later, by a second, in which a " London and Bristol Railway," with extensions to Oxford, Cheltenham, Gloucester, Taunton, Exeter and Falmouth was foreshadowed. Both these documents were signed by a Mr. Henry Price and a Mr. William Brunton, and may be described as unofficial.

Early in 1833 a Committee appointed by the society of Merchant Adventurers, the Bristol Chamber of Commerce, and other local bodies, reported that it had discussed the construction of a line to London, and was in favour of it. The public bodies concerned then advanced money

An interesting letter from Mr. I. K. Brunel to Mr Michael Lane, a former Engineer-in-Chief of the Great Western Railway.

is shown by an incident that happened just before his election. On hearing that some members of the committee of selection had decided to give the post to the engineer who would put in the lowest estimate for the line, Brunel at once wished to withdraw his name. For, as he justly pointed out, such a criterion merely put a premium on flattering promises, and would appeal most to the man who had least reputation to lose, and cared least about losing what he had already.

Brunel had extraordinary keenness of mind, perseverance, and originality, with an inclination to doing things on the grand scale. In addition he had immense capacity for hard work, otherwise he could not have carried through in 40 years the many enterprises with which he was associated or for which he was responsible. As a bridge-builder he was in the highest class. The structures at Saltash, Chepstow and elsewhere would have made him famous, apart from railways and shipbuilding. While engaged on his multifarious railway activities he found time for making remarkable experiments in steam navigation. Thus, during the construction of the first section of the Great Western Railway he designed and overlooked the building of the " Great Western " steamship, the first to be constructed for regular Transatlantic service. The next few years saw him busy with the " Great Britain," the first large steamship to be built of iron and driven by a screw propeller. Simultaneously with the construction of the South Wales Railway he brought into being the " Great Eastern," one of the greatest engineering ventures of the Victorian Age, which, though commercially a failure, triumphantly vindicated new and much criticised constructional principles.* His success as a shipbuilder has been well summed up thus :—" The conclusions he sought to establish are now so generally accepted that it is difficult to believe that they were even questioned. No one now has any doubt that large vessels can with safety be built of iron, or that the screw propeller can be advantageously employed in ships of war and the mercantile navy ; no one can now deny that it is practicable for steamships to make long voyages across the ocean with regularity and speed."†

Brunel had great influence on the acceptance of Sir Joseph Paxton's designs for the great building to house the Exhibition of 1851, now known as the Crystal Palace. When the structure was removed to Sydenham, Brunel designed the two lofty water towers, which are so conspicuous a feature of it. At various times the great engineer carried out dock and harbour works—at Bristol, Portishead, Plymouth, Briton Ferry, Brentford and Milford Haven. He also interested himself in gunnery and ballistics, and during the Crimean War designed military hospitals on a new principle—the pavilion—for shipping to Renkioi, on the Dardanelles. His versatility is well illustrated by this incursion into the field of medicine, for the success of the special arrangements adopted by him caused the Americans to construct similar hospitals during the Civil War, and the Germans to do so during the Franco Prussian War : and, we might add, most nations to follow suit in the Great War.

* Such as longitudinal framing, cellular double bottom, and subdivision of hull by bulkheads.—A.W.

† Life of I. K. Brunel, by his Son.

BRUNEL AND AFTER

Brunel apparently led a charmed life, for on several occasions his life was in great danger. The Thames Tunnel episode has already been referred to. In 1838, while aboard the " Great Western," he fell down a ladder, and was found unconscious on his face in a pool of water. Twice he was nearly killed on the Great Western Railway : and he had yet another escape when he swallowed a half-sovereign which, after being six weeks in his windpipe, was at last extracted by means of an apparatus designed by the engineer himself. The patient was attached to an enlarged edition of a looking-glass frame and quickly inverted. After several attempts the coin fell into his mouth. While his life was in danger public excitement was intense, so high was his place in public estimation ; and when at last the news went round : " It is out," the whole country drew a sigh of relief.

PRELIMINARY SURVEY

Immediately after his appointment Brunel began a preliminary survey, and such was his energy that, within a month, he had reconnoitred and mapped out a route from Bristol to London.

Soon after his report was handed in, the Committee called, on July 30, 1833, the first public meeting for the purpose of forming a Company to construct the railway, and of appointing a Board of Management, which could consist of a body of Bristol Directors and a similar body of London Directors—forty persons in all.

The Board met for the first time on August 19, 1833, in London, and at this meeting the title, " Great Western Railway," was first used officially.

8

The Room in which the Great Western Railway was " born."

BRUNEL AND AFTER

Brunel had now to make a detailed survey preparatory to the presentation of a Bill to Parliament. He divided the work up among a number of assistants—the finding of capable helpers was a difficult task in those days—and spent several weeks travelling about the country and generally directing operations. During this time he took hardly any rest: " I am rarely much under twenty hours a day at it," he wrote to a friend, and his diary shows that he often sat up writing reports until it was almost time for him to mount his horse and ride away to the next day's work. Such sleep as he got was frequently taken in his armchair. In addition to keeping a watchful eye on the surveying operations, there fell upon Brunel the necessity for conciliating the landowners over whose property his assistants needed to work. In the latter task he was assisted by his tact and good humour, which, combined with a cheerful and joyous disposition, gave him the enviable quality of being able to make friends wherever he went.

The first Prospectus of the Great Western Railway appeared in 1833. It urged as the main object of the railway the facilities that it would offer for moving merchandise; but also pointed out that a good revenue should accrue from passenger traffic. In this connection it mentioned that the passenger-miles travelled on the Great Western (Bath) road in a year totalled 544,352. The map accompanying the 1834 prospectus shows a projected line from Merthyr Tydvil to Cardiff; as the Directors evidently had their eyes on the matter of a coal supply for the locomotives to be used.

THE ROUTE SELECTED

In laying out a path for the proposed railway between Reading and Bath, Brunel had the choice of going either south or north of the Marlborough Downs. He took the northerly course for two reasons. In the first place, it permitted easier gradients and gentler curves, both of which were very important for the high speed of travel which he had always in mind ; and in the second, it would give easy extensions to Oxford, Gloucester, and other important towns, and a more convenient way into South Wales. By following the Thames west of Reading, the railway would pass through a gorge between the Chilterns on the north and the Berkshire Downs on the south, and turn the flank of the latter. For a distance of 77 miles the rails would rise westwards almost imperceptibly, on gradients nowhere exceeding 8 feet, and seldom exceeding 5 feet, per mile, to Swindon, 253 feet higher than the London terminus. The fall to Bristol was to be concentrated mainly into two gradients of 1 in 100—one at Wootton Bassett and the other in a tunnel (the Box) driven through the south-western end of the Cotswolds. If necessary, these gradients would be worked by auxiliary power.

The Directors approved the route taken by Brunel ; George Stephenson himself admitted it to be the best possible ; and present-day opinion also upholds it. Meetings were called at Bath, Windsor and other places to interest the public in the scheme and overcome opposition, but, as subscriptions fell far short of expectations, it was determined in the first instance to seek powers to make railways from Bath to Bristol and from London to Reading " as a means of facilitating the ultimate establishment of a railway between London and Bristol." Application for sanction to lay rails from Reading to Bath was to be left till a future occasion. In the meanwhile the Kennet and Avon Canal would have to serve as the connecting link. The most troublesome portions of the through navigation would be superseded if the Bill went through ; and in any case half a loaf was better than no bread.

THE G.W.R. IN PARLIAMENT

The Bill passed the second reading in the House of Commons and went into Committee, where all sorts of the usual and special objections against a railway were raised by witnesses—some of them quite ridiculous. It would poison the air. It would spoil the landscape. It would interfere with drainage. It would deprive the Thames of its traffic and cause the river to become choked. It would corrupt the morals of Eton boys by giving them easy access to the dissipations of London ; and so on. More solid opposition came from the coaching interests and the landowners, the latter in many cases refusing to see that the railway would increase, rather than decrease, the value of property it passed through. Brunel's proposal to have the terminus at the north end of Vauxhall Bridge encountered such hostility that the promoters moved its location further west to South Kensington. Even that concession did not ward off attack, as the Kensingtonians with the greatest energy opposed having a terminus in their midst.

BILL REJECTED

After 54 days had been occupied in hearing evidence—eleven of them in cross-examining Brunel, who acquitted himself in a manner that aroused general admiration—the Bill was passed. On reaching the Upper House, however, it was thrown out, by 47 votes to 30, several of the peers voting against it because they were in favour of a complete scheme, not of one which, as was sarcastically said, " would be a head and a tail without a body, and neither ' Great ' nor ' Western,' nor even a railway at all."

The Directors took the hint, and, not the least daunted by defeat, prepared to bring in another Bill in the following year, 1835. Fortunately they were able, during the later months of 1834, to raise sufficient money to finance the whole of a line from London to Bristol.

The Supplementary Prospectus, dated September, 1834, which appeared after the rejection of the Bill, contains a passage that is worth quoting :

" As reference to the map might lead to the enquiry why a line by way of Hungerford, Devizes and Bradford was not chosen, it is right to state that a survey of that district was in the first instance made, but the difficulty and expense of such a railway, owing to the altitude of the general levels of the country, were found to be so considerable that, even without reference to the reasons already adduced, the Directors cannot hesitate to prefer the Northern line, which will scarcely exceed the other in length, and which, embracing Oxford, the clothing districts of Gloucestershire, the important towns of Stroud, Cheltenham and Gloucester, and thence leading eventually to Wales, might also be made to communicate, by a short branch, as before stated, with Bradford, Trowbridge and other manufacturing towns on the Southern line."

It is interesting to read in the same document that the number of people using the road between London and Reading was proved to be greater than on any other road of equal length in England.

To get over the terminus difficulty, arrangements were made with the London and Birmingham (afterwards the London and North Western) Railway to join up with that line a little west of the Kensal Green Cemetery (where to this day the two lines are but $\frac{1}{3}$ mile apart), and use Euston as a common terminal.

In the first Bill the gauge proposed was the ordinary gauge of 4 feet $8\frac{1}{2}$ inches. In the second, no mention at all of gauge was made, at Brunel's special request, because he had already in mind a gauge of more generous dimensions.

The Bill met with as much opposition as its predecessor. The Box Tunnel, on account of its great length, was labelled " dangerous," " impracticable," " monstrous," and so on, by opponents ; and George Stephenson, called to give evidence, was put through a severe cross-examination with regard to its feasibility. " Old George," however, expressed his complete agreement with Brunel, and laughed at any likelihood of passengers being smothered by fumes from the engine. The enemy then attacked the selected route as a whole, arguing that the southern one, though not so level as the northern, could have its gradients so balanced that in effect they would cancel one another out. This drew from the Chairman of Committee, Lord Wharncliffe, the sarcastic comment that, if the principle were sound, the Highlands of Scotland would be ideal for a railway !

Eventually the Bill was read a third time, and four months later Brunel wrote in his Diary : " The railway now is in progress. I am thus engineer to the finest work in England. But what a fight we have had, and how near defeat, and what a ruinous defeat it would have been ! It is like looking back upon a fearful pass ; but we have succeeded."

Soon after the Royal Assent had been obtained the Directors had a census taken of traffic on the two main roads with which the Great Western would compete. Observers were stationed at Colnbrook, on the Bath Road, and at Hanwell, on the Uxbridge Road, to keep tally of everything that passed. The figures recorded were as follows :—

	COLNBROOK	HANWELL	TOTAL
Stage Coaches - -	77	46	123
Post Chaises and Private Carriages - -	105	38	143
Mounted Saddle Horses	78	27	105
Phætons and Gigs -	95	45	140
Spring Carts - -	52	29	81
Stage Carts - -	29	47	76
Waggons - - -	80	52	132
	516	284	800

The Colnbrook observers also scored 75 pigs, 740 sheep, and 110 cattle ; but the Hanwell records do not include livestock. In connection with the last it may be mentioned that, prior to railway days, livestock had to come to London " on the hoof." Enormous numbers of cattle, sheep, and pigs blocked the main roads at certain seasons, and there may still be seen in several parts of the country " cattle drives "—unmetalled lanes, with trees on either side— used by the old drovers. This method of transport caused much suffering to the animals and loss to the owners. Mr. George Bowlby, a London salesman, who gave evidence in 1834 in favour of a railway from London to Bristol, stated that, of the pigs bought by him at Bristol, from 40 to 50 died every week on the road to London ; and that, owing to the poor condition of animals generally after a long journey on foot, their meat fetched from three farthings to a penny less than that of country-killed animals.

CHAPTER THE SECOND

THE ADVANCE OF THE RAILS

THE news of the incorporation of the Great Western Railway was received with rejoicing in Bristol and London. For the first city it heralded a new era of prosperity : for the second cheaper supplies of many kinds, and much easier communication with a very important area of the country.

Before many months had passed, contracts had been let for a good part of the construction, and the countryside was invaded by gangs of navvies, the successors of the " navigators " who, in the previous 70 years, had criss-crossed England with her canal system. A nucleus of the old canal hands proved invaluable to the builders of our early railways, owing to the practical knowledge these men had of the nature and behaviour of various soils and rocks, and of making embankments and cuttings. The picture that Samuel Smiles draws of the navvy of this period is as follows : " He usually wore a white felt hat with the brim turned up, a velveteen or jean square-tailed coat, a scarlet plush waistcoat with little black spots, and a bright-coloured 'kerchief round his herculean neck, when, as often happened, it was not left entirely bare. His corduroy breeches were retained in position by a leathern strap round the waist, and were tied and buttoned at the knee, displaying beneath a solid calf and foot encased in strong high-laced boots. . . . . Their powers of endurance were extraordinary. In times of emergency they would work for 12 or even 16 hours, with only short intervals for meals. The quantity of flesh-meat which they consumed was something enormous ; but it was to their bones and muscles what coke is to the locomotive—the means of keeping up steam. Working, eating, drinking, and sleeping together, and daily exposed to the same influences, these railway labourers soon presented a distinct and well-defined character, strongly marking them from the population of the districts in which they laboured. Reckless alike of their lives as of their earnings, the navvies worked hard and lived hard. For their lodging a hut of turf would content them, and, in their hours of leisure, the meanest public house would serve for their parlour."

In those days there were no steam-diggers nor other labour-saving devices for railway work, and human muscles had to do much of what now is done by mechanical power. The English navvy responded to the demands on his energy, and to this fact may be attributed the extraordinary rapidity, considering all the difficulties to be overcome, with which the early railways were completed.

LONDON TO READING

On the first division of the line—from London to Reading—the chief obstacles to be surmounted were the Brent Valley, at Hanwell, the River Thames, at Maidenhead, and the hill between Twyford and Sonning. The first is negotiated by the Wharncliffe Viaduct—named after Lord Wharncliffe, Chairman of the Committee that decided in the House of Lords the fate of the Great Western Railway Bill. The Viaduct, which cost £40,000

The Wharncliffe Viaduct, Hanwell.

to build, and has a length of about 900 feet, and a maximum height of 65 feet, is a brickwork structure with eight semi-elliptical arches of 70 feet span, supported on twin hollow piers. Westward of the viaduct the track crossed the main Oxford road by a cast iron bridge, which in 1847 was so damaged by a fire that Brunel replaced it with one of wrought iron. Beyond the bridge an embankment ¾ mile long was needed to maintain the grade, which in this section is practically level. Some trouble was caused by settlements of this embankment, until proper drains were used.

The Thames offered a more difficult problem, for at the point where it had to be crossed it is about 100 yards wide. Fortunately, there was a shoal in mid-stream convenient for a central pier, and Brunel decided on a brick bridge having two main spans of 128 feet of semi-elliptical form, with a rise of only 24¼ feet, and four brick approach arches at

Maidenhead Bridge.

either end.   Maidenhead bridge is remarkable as including
the longeſt—certainly the flatteſt—spans ever carried out
in brickwork.   Their flatness aroused a good deal of criticism as soon as the designs were published, and the
contraċtor became so alarmed that he wished to be relieved
from his contraċt.   Brunel, however, persuaded him, by
means of some simple geometrical diagrams, that there was
no cause for anxiety, and the work proceeded.   Owing to
the centering of the eaſtern span being removed before the
cement had hardened sufficiently, a slight extra flattening
took place ;   but Brunel's calculations have been amply
juſtified by the bridge having carried ſteadily increasing
loads for nearly ninety years.   When its width was doubled
in 1893, the new conſtruċtion was built on exaċtly the same
lines as the old.

The high ground between Twyford and Reading was,
according to the original plans, to be pierced by a tunnel,
but a cutting was subſtituted.   This entailed a great deal of

heavy work, as its length is over two miles and its depth varies from 20 to 60 feet; but the material excavated came in useful for the embankments at both ends of the cutting.

THE BROAD GAUGE

Brunel had laid out the line for high speed, and was not at all satisfied that this could be attained with safety on what was afterwards regarded as the " narrow " gauge— now the standard gauge—of 4 feet 8½ inches. In a report to the Directors, dated October, 1835, he recommended a gauge of 7 feet.* This would allow the carriages to be placed between, instead of over the wheels, and increase their steadiness by lowering the centre of gravity. Also, the wheels could then be of large size, and their axles, turning at a low speed, would set up comparative little friction. Another consideration which weighed with him was the facility that a wide gauge would give for building powerful engines, with easily accessible machinery.

The Directors approved his suggestions; which were followed, a few months later, by others urging some radical deviations from the then accepted methods of tracklaying. With an eye to obtaining the most perfect running surface possible, he advocated timber instead of stone blocks as the supports for the rails, the support to be given *continuously* by heavy longitudinal baulks, to which rails of " bridge " section would be bolted without the interposition of chairs. At intervals the longitudinals were to be supported on cross-pieces, called transoms, which would keep the rails the correct distance apart. This was in reality

* *To be exact, 7ft. 0¼in.—A.W.*

a reversion to the method used for the original wooden tramways.

To hold the track steady, Brunel had piles driven down into solid ground between the rails. The transoms were in pairs, one on each side of the pile, into which they were shouldered, long bolts holding the three parts together.

The construction period was full of anxieties for the Directors, since the difficulties which are inseparable from railway construction even in these days were then aggravated by lack of experience on the part of the engineers, who may be described as experimenters on a huge scale.

PADDINGTON AS TERMINUS

We get some very interesting " peeps behind the scenes " in the diary kept by one of the original Directors, Mr. George Henry Gibbs, during the period March, 1836, till May, 1840 (excepting for a gap of 13 months from June, 1836, onwards). One of the first subjects referred to in the Diary concerns the London terminus. By the Act of 1835 this was to be at Euston, under an agreement previously come to with the London and Birmingham (afterwards the London and North Western) Railway to share that station. A junction was to be made near Kensal Green Cemetery, where the two railways are to-day but a third of a mile apart. However, as the result of friction between the companies, the Great Western Railway Directors decided, in 1836, to have a terminus of their own, and selected for it a site in the then countrified outlying suburb of Paddington, about half a mile west of the present station. As if in anticipation, Walter Hancock inaugurated in the same year a steam-coach service between Paddington, the Bank, and

Stratford. The coaches ran continuously for five months, averaged 5¼ hours' travel daily, and in 600 trips covered 4,200 miles, carrying several thousands of passengers.

This change in plans caused complications, as deviation from the original route would mean obtaining, first, permission from landowners and others to carry the rails through their properties, and then Parliamentary sanction. Construction as far east as Acton was already well under way, and in their anxiety not to hold up the opening of the line the Directors decided, as soon as property owners had been settled with, to " take a risk " as regards Parliament, and push the work ahead towards Paddington while leave was being asked. Should an Act not be obtained, the Company would be out of pocket by from twenty-five to fifty thousands of pounds ; if it were, some six months' time would have been saved. Fortunately, the necessary Act was passed without difficulty ; but the Directors must have had their anxious moments about it.

The old Paddington station was quite a small building. A contributor to the *Railway Magazine* writes of it in 1838 : " The entrance gate and piers, with a gatekeeper's lodge in the centre, are substantial, and sufficient without any pretensions to splendour. An excellent road for carriages, with a broad pavement for foot passengers, leads to the centre of the Station, on the right hand side of which is a capacious enginehouse and carriage sheds, better designed than any I have before seen ; on the left side a wide space is left, apparently for a merchandise station, and a further space nearer the Paddington Canal, which is, I presume, intended for shipping docks for forwarding goods by canal to the Thames, and the London and other docks."

Old Paddington Station, 1850.

24

It was replaced in 1854 by part of the present station at a cost of £534,000. The interior of the principal part of the station as then completed was 700 feet long, and 238 feet wide, divided in its width by two rows of columns into three spans, 68, 102 and 68 feet wide. The design, for which Brunel was responsible, lent itself admirably to extensions, and gave the Great Western what is still the most conveniently arranged of the large London terminals.

The Great Western Hotel, built at the end of the land belonging to the Company, was opened at the same time as the station. But it proved itself a " white elephant," as no tenant could be found for it. Eventually a few of the shareholders formed a company to lease and work the hotel, and of this Brunel was first a director and then the Chairman, a post which he held till his death. With the extension of the Great Western Railway system more and more business accrued to the hotel, until it became a very flourishing concern. In 1896 the lease expired, and the hotel has since been managed by the railway authorities.

By the end of 1837 the opening of the London-Maidenhead section was in sight, and the question of the fares to be charged came under consideration. The author of the Diary thought : " that prices should be low enough decidedly to exclude the competition of coaches and to secure the multiplication of travellers on which we have relied so much, and as low as we can go consistently with the probability of our being able by-and-by to reduce them still further. Coaches to Maidenhead are now 8s. to 10s. inside, 4s. to 5s. outside. We can safely charge 5s., 4s., and 3s., all under cover."

At this period the Directorate appears to have been subjected to a great deal of criticism from a body of Liverpool shareholders, who, perhaps naturally, favoured the gauge and methods of tracklaying employed by Stephenson for the successful Liverpool and Manchester Railway, and were anxious to be represented on the Board. But such distractions did not prevent operations being pushed ahead as fast as the many obstacles to be overcome permitted. It is difficult for us to realise how much thought had then to be given to details that to-day would be decided with but little trouble. The whole organisation had to be built up from the very beginning. More or less untried men must be assigned to various posts, high and low. A system of keeping the track in order needed evolving. The rolling stock required planning and experimenting with : it was not a matter of merely placing an order with some large loco-motive, carriage or wagon works, as may be done by any new line opened to-day. We can, therefore, easily understand that those responsible had a hard and worrying time of it while the right way of doing things was being discovered.

The completion of the first section of the Great Western Railway was awaited with the utmost interest, not merely as marking the first stage in a great enterprise, but because the track was a challenge to ordinary practice. " Among all the great lines in this country," said the *Railway Magazine* of those days, " not even excepting our good and great railway Adam, the Liverpool and Manchester, no one has ever more intensely concentrated public opinion upon it than the Great Western. Neither is this confined to England. France, Germany, Italy, etc., are all looking forward with the greatest interest to the opening of the line, as the period which is to decide a question as important to railways as the introduction of them has been to civilised Europe. . . . . . A short time will now settle the question, and decide whether Mr. Brunel's plans are worthy to be followed or not."

FIRST SECTION OF G.W.R. OPENED

The date of opening to the public the Paddington to Maidenhead—or more properly to Taplow, as the bridge was not yet finished—section was finally fixed for June 4, 1838. The first locomotive, the "Vulcan," had in January been put on the rails at West Drayton, to which

" North Star."

point it was brought by canal; and in the meantime the " North Star " had reached Maidenhead by water. On the last day of May the Directors and about two hundred guests took a preliminary trip over the railway in special trains.

Great Western Railway.
LONDON TO MAIDENHEAD.

a d 1839.

On and after the 1st of May, the SOUTHALL STATION will be opened
For Passengers and Parcels.

An **Extra Train to Slough** will leave Paddington on **Sunday Mornings**, at half-past 9 o'clock, calling at Ealing, Hanwell, Southall and West Drayton.

Horses and Carriages, being at the Paddington or Maidenhead Station ten minutes before the departure of a Train, will be conveyed upon this Railway.

Charge for 4-wheel Carriage, 12s. *Two-wheel ditto*, 8s. *For 1 Horse*, 10s. *Pair of Horses*, 16s.

Post Horses are kept in readiness both at Paddington and Maidenhead, and upon sufficient notice being given at Paddington, or at the Bull and Mouth Office, St. Martin's-le-Grand, would be sent to bring Carriages from any part of London to the station, at a moderate charge.

TRAINS.

From Paddington	To Maidenhead.		From Maidenhead	To Paddington.
8 o'clock morn. calling at	Southall and Slough		6 o'clock morning, calling at	Slough
9 do.	Slough			(and on Wednesday Morning at Southall)
10 do.	West Drayton and Slough		8 do.	Slough and West Drayton
12 do.	West Drayton and Slough		9 do.	Slough and West Drayton
3 o'clock afternoon	West Drayton and Slough		10 do.	Slough and Southall
4 do.			12 do.	Slough and West Drayton
5 do.	Hanwell and Slough		3 o'clock afternoon	Slough and Southall
6 o'clock evening	Ealing, West Drayton and Slough		4 do.	Slough
7 do.	Southall and Slough		6 o'clock evening	Slough and Hanwell
8 do.	Slough		6 do.	Slough and West Drayton
			7 do.	Slough and Ealing

The six o'clock up Train will call at Southall on Wednesday mornings, for the convenience of persons attending the market on that day.

SHORT TRAINS.

From Paddington	To West Drayton			From West Drayton	To Paddington.	
½ past 9 o'Clock Morning,		calling at	Ealing,	before 9 o'Clock Morning,		calling at Southall,
½ past 1 do. Afternoon,			Hanwell,	before 11 do.		Hanwell,
½ past 4 do. do.			AND	before 3 do. Afternoon		AND
½ past 8 do. Evening,			Southall,	before 7 o'Clock Evening		Ealing.

☞ There are no second class close carriages in the short Trains.

Passengers and Parcels for Slough and Maidenhead will be conveyed from all the stations by means of the short Trains, waiting to be taken on by the succeeding long Train, as above; and in like manner they will be conveyed from Maidenhead and Slough, to every station on the Line.

On SUNDAYS.

From Paddington	To Maidenhead.		From Maidenhead	To Paddington.
8 o'clock Morn. calling at	Ealing and Slough		6 o'clock morn. calling at	Slough
½ past 9 do.	West Drayton and Slough		8 do.	Slough Southall and Ealing
3 do.	Southall and Slough		9 do.	Slough West Drayton and Hanwell
5 afternoon do.	Hanwell West Drayton and Slough		3 afternoon do.	Slough and Hanwell
7 evening do.	Ealing West Drayton and Slough		5 evening do.	Slough and West Drayton
8 do.	Southall and Slough		7 do.	Slough and Ealing

SHORT TRAINS,
PADDINGTON TO SLOUGH.

Half-past Nine o'Clock Morning, - - - - calling at Ealing, Hanwell, Southall, and Drayton.

To West Drayton.			From West Drayton.		
½ past 9 o'Clock Morning,	calling at	Ealing, Hanwell, & Southall, and proceeding to Slough	before 8 o'Clock Morning,	calling at	Southall, Hanwell & Ealing.
½ past 8 do. Evening,		Ealing, Hanwell & Southall	before 5 do. Evening,		

FARES.

Paddington.	1st. Class. Coach.	Second Class. Close.	Second Class. Open.	Maidenhead.	1st. Class. Coach.	Second Class. Close.	Second Class. Open.
To Ealing	1 6	1 0	0 9	To Slough	2 0	1 6	1 0
Hanwell	2 0	1 6	1 0	West Drayton	3 0	2 6	2 0
Southall	2 6	1 9	1 3	Southall	4 0	3 0	2 6
West Drayton	3 6	2 0	1 6	Hanwell ...	4 6	3 6	3 0
Slough	4 6	3 0	2 0	Ealing	5 0	4 0	3 6
Maidenhead,..	5 6	4 0	3 6	Paddington.	5 6	4 0	3 6

The same Fares will be charged from Slough to West Drayton as from Maidenhead to Slough.

Omnibuses and Coaches start from Princes Street, Bank, one hour before the departure of each Train, calling at the Angel Inn, Islington; Bull Inn, Holborn; Moore's Green Man and still, Oxford Street; Golden Cross, Charing Cross; Chaplin's Universal Office, Regent Circus; and Gloucester Warehouse, Oxford Street; to the Paddington station.—Fare 6d. without Luggage.

J. Robinson, Printer, Maidenhead.

The First Great Western Time Table, A.D. 1839.

The down journey was made in 49 minutes, or at about 28 miles an hour, while the return run averaged 33½ miles an hour.   On June 2nd, the Eton College authorities applied for an injunction to prevent stopping at Slough, but this was dismissed, with costs, as *stopping* did not violate the condition that a station was not to be provided at Slough.

The formal opening was carried out according to schedule.   The first public train consisted of three first-class and five second-class coaches, and a truck carrying a post chaise.   In it rode the author of the Diary, from which we take the following : " June 4th.—Our railway opened to the public this morning.   I went to Maidenhead by the first train and came back by the third, which started from Maidenhead at 10.15.   I was disappointed with regard to the speed, as we were 1 hour and 20 minutes going down and 1 hour and five minutes coming up.   If from the 65 minutes we deduct 4 lost at Drayton, 3 at Slough, and 4 between the two places, and in slackening and getting up the speed, there remain 54 minutes for 23 miles, or 25½ miles per hour.   We carried altogether to-day 1,479 people, and took £226."

The occasion did not prove a great success from the running point of view, as the track showed a certain bumpiness which had caused some anxiety ever since the rails had been laid.   The trouble appears to have been due in part to the imperfections of the carriage springs,* but more particularly to the piles used to steady the track.   The passage of the trains naturally consolidated the, as yet, more or less loose ballast under the longitudinal timbers,

* *As these were of springless iron their inefficiency is not to be wondered at.—A.W.*

29

which could not bed themselves properly owing to the rigid support given at intervals by the piles. Consequently, the track tended to produce the effect of one having rails laid on very widely spaced sleepers.

INTERNAL DISSENSIONS

The Liverpool contingent now became very critical and threatened to call a special meeting to go into the matter of the gauge and track. To anticipate them, the Directors decided to get a " second opinion," and called in Mr. Nicholas Wood, of Stockton and Darlington Railway fame, and Mr. (afterwards Sir) John Hawkshaw, the future engineer of the Severn Tunnel. The first condemned the piling system; the second advocated the abandonment of the broad gauge, and Brunel's whole system of tracklaying, and strongly advised the Directors to scrap their existing rolling stock. The cost of altering the gauge to Maidenhead and of providing new stock he estimated at £124,000. Brunel, who had passed through a very unhappy time since the opening of the railway, presented a report in reply to those of the advisory experts ; and said that, if it were necessary, he would abandon his methods. But he refused to work in association with another engineer, and insisted on resigning if any appointment were made which should mean dual control of the engineering department.

A special meeting of shareholders having been called for January 9, 1839, to consider the three reports, the Directors, who had resolved to stand by Brunel, secured all the proxies they could possibly get hold of. As a result the Directorate obtained a majority of 1645 on a motion that the broad gauge should be retained, along with the longitudinal system of supporting the rails, but the use of piles be abolished. This momentous decision definitely committed the Great Western Railway to the broad gauge and to the subsequent extra expenditure of millions of pounds on the tracks laid to that gauge. The track, as far as Taplow, had to be reconditioned, at a cost to the Company of nearly £100,000. All the piles were removed or driven down ; and the transoms placed between, instead of under, the longitudinals, to which they were secured by strap bolts, the timber work thus resembling a ladder with very widely spaced rungs, laid flat on the ground.

Meanwhile the traffic returns had not been discouraging. For the first three weeks the number of passengers carried averaged 10,000 weekly ; and this figure was maintained till the end of the year. The Seventh half-yearly Report of the Company states that 264,644 passengers had used the railway up to December 31, 1838. It also mentions that the mail and long-distance coaches to Cheltenham, Oxford, Bath and Bristol were still using the roads right through to London, owing to the short distance of line yet opened. It afterwards became the practice, as the line was extended, for coaches to be carried between railhead and London on flat trucks, the passengers presumably retaining their seats—the " inside " ones, at any rate. That the railway was rapidly overcoming prejudice is shown by an application being received, within a month of the opening, from the Eton masters for a special train to take the boys up to town. The " corrupting " powers of the railway appear to have been forgotten somewhat quickly !

In 1839, as soon as the Maidenhead bridge had been

completed, the railway was opened to Twyford. The Sonning cutting was giving a good deal of trouble and the contractor not carrying out his contract satisfactorily. Bad weather hindered operations both here and between Bristol

Old Reading Station

and Bath, as also in the large cuttings near Chippenham. The year 1840, however, saw a considerable extension of the line, for it reached Reading on March 31, Steventon on June 1, Challow (then called Faringdon Road) on July 20, and Hay Lane, near Wootton Bassett, on December 16. At the other end, the Bristol to Bath section, which included several tunnels and generally a great deal of heavy work, was opened on June 20, so that by the close of the year only about 24 miles, out of $118\frac{3}{4}$, remained unfinished. This stretch included by far the greatest engineering work on the line, the Box Tunnel, which is 1 mile 7 furlongs in length, and cost £100 per yard to drive. It was easily the longest railway tunnel of its time, though many longer have been driven in England since. Like other tunnels for the broad-gauge double tracks, it is 30 feet wide at the spring of the arch, and the crown is 25 feet above the rails, which lie 7 feet above the invert. To provide good ventilation, Brunel sank six shafts, 30 feet in diameter, and from 70 to 300 feet deep, on the line of the tunnel, and used them as bases from which to carry on the excavation. This presented no serious difficulties, as the materials to be pierced were Bath Stone and a stiff marl. A leading geologist and friend of Brunel, after the completion of the tunnel, thought fit publicly to question its safety, and the engineer, who took little notice of ordinary gossip, wrote him a somewhat caustic letter, asking him, in so many words, why he did not give him advice while the work was in operation, instead of waiting till the only effect of his pronouncement would be to scare the public and injure the railway. Brunel, however, had no doubts as to the safety of the tunnel, though the prospect of passing through one of such great length was at first so terrible to some travellers that they preferred to post along the turnpike road overhead and await a train at the further end.

On May 31, 1841, trains were running from London to Chippenham, and on June 30, to Bristol. Thus, in nine years the desire of the Bristolians was fulfilled, and a new highway opened which revolutionised communication between east and west. The coaching establishments, indeed, fell on evil days, celebrated inns decayed, and great stables which once held hundreds of horses stood empty ; while for the high roads began a period of neglect.   To arrive at

Bristol Station, 1840.

a correct estimate of how far the public gained by the changeover from road and horse to rail and steam, we cannot do better than give some figures contained in the first half-yearly Report issued after the opening of the whole line.   According to this the number of passengers that used the line during the last six months of 1841 was 882,119, and the total of passenger-miles travelled 27,538,760, or 32½ miles per journey. With these we may compare the 544,352 passenger-miles of travellers on coaches along the Bath Road, as stated in the Prospectus of 1834 (see p. 10). The sudden increase of travel by 5,000 per cent. in a few years tells its own story.

THE G.W.R. AND THE PRESS

Nowadays the opening of a new railway or an extension of an old one in this country may pass almoſt unnoticed. Eighty-five years ago it attracted as much attention as the completion of the firſt line in a new country. We do not read of any processions on the Great Weſtern such as marked the opening of the Stockton and Darlington and the Liverpool and Mancheſter railways. But it is intereſting to take a peep or two, through the medium of the Press, at the reception of the new trunk line by the populace along its route.

By the courtesy of the Editor of the *Reading Mercury and Oxford Gazette*, we are permitted to extract a few quotations bearing on the subject. The issue of March 14,

" Fire Fly."

1840, says under the caption, " Further Extension of the Great Western Railway to Reading " :—

" This line was opened to the Reading public on Monday morning last, when the first train, drawn by the " Fire Fly," started from Paddington at six o'clock. The novelty of this delightful and expeditious mode of travelling, coupled with the extreme beauty of the morning, attracted a vast number of our country friends to the town. Indeed, we have seldom witnessed a greater influx of visitors. At the Station-house every accommodation was afforded the spectators which could reasonably be expected or desired by them, the extensive platform immediately adjoining the office having been thrown open to the public, and seats provided, in a most handsome manner for their convenience. Trains were progressing to and fro at all hours of the day, and the passengers were quite as numerous as could have been expected at the commencement, as some of the Bristol [stage] coaches have not yet made Reading their terminus : an increase, however, may be shortly relied on . . . . In the course of the afternoon, several thousands of lookers-on were congregated on Forbury Hill, and in the immediate vicinity of the railroad. The distance between this and Paddington Station is 35¾ miles, and the time occupied in completing the same, including four or five stoppages, may be averaged at one hour and a quarter. A new and powerful engine, named the 'Wild Fire,' made its debut yesterday, occupying one hour ten minutes in its journey, and on Thursday one of the engines completed the whole distance in one hour five minutes . . . . It is now become a prevailing topic of conversation with many, whether from the opening of the Railway, Reading will experience benefit or injury."

The last sentence suggests the coaching interests being up in arms. However, in the issue of a fortnight later we read that : " The trains of the Great Western Railway yesterday were crowded to an unparalleled extent; it was calculated that, in the course of the day, nearly 4,000 persons left the station at Paddington for Slough and the intermediate stations between Paddington and Reading. The seven o'clock up-train from this town required two engines, all thirteen carriages being filled." So evidently public opinion had soon sided with the railway.

Further down the line the country folk gave the railway an unequivocal welcome. To quote from the June 6, 1840, issue of the same journal :

" *Opening of the Great Western Railway to Steventon.*"

" From an early hour on Monday every road in the direction of Steventon was crowded with passengers. Oxford and Abingdon, and the adjacent towns and villages poured forth their inhabitants in droves, every description of vehicle seemed in requisition on the occasion, and multitudes of pedestrians were found on the way to witness the triumphant results of scientific enterprise. So large a concourse of persons, we may safely say, has not been brought together in this part of the country for many years as was witnessed at Steventon on Monday last, and all from the youngest to the most aged spectator there appeared struck with astonishment at this novel and rapid mode of communication."

THE ELECTRIC TELEGRAPH

Two years before the completion of the railway the

Directors gave proof of their care for the safety of the public travelling " Great Western " by installing Cooke and Wheatstone's system of telegraphic communication between Paddington and West Drayton. This was the very first telegraph line of considerable length to be put into use. The three wires needed to work it were carried in an iron tube attached to short posts beside the line. By 1844 it had been extended to Slough, whence a message was dispatched on August 6, announcing the birth of Prince Alfred at Windsor Castle. A special train brought Sir Robert Peel and Lord Stanley from Paddington to Slough in 18 minutes, while a second did the distance of 18 miles in half a minute less. This latter carried the Duke of Wellington, who had taken very reluctantly to railway travelling. It would be interesting to know what he thought of the " going."

The first use of the telegraph for police purposes happened in the same year on the Eton Montem Day—which seems to have had somewhat of a race-meeting attraction for light-fingered gentry.

In the telegraph book then kept at Paddington Station may be found the following passages relating to that day :

" PADDINGTON, 10.20 a.m.—Mail train just started. It contains three thieves, named Sparrow, Burrell, and Spurgeon, in the first compartment of the fourth first-class carriage.

" SLOUGH, 10.50 a.m.—Mail train arrived. The officers have cautioned the three thieves.

" PADDINGTON, 10.50 a.m.—Special train just left. It contained two thieves ; one named Oliver Martin, who is dressed in black, crape on his hat ; the other named Fiddler

Dick, in black trousers and light blouse. Both in the third compartment of the first second-class carriage.

" SLOUGH, 11.16 a.m.—Special train arrived. Officers have taken the two thieves into custody, a lady having lost her bag, containing a purse with two sovereigns and some silver in it ; one of the sovereigns was sworn to by the lady as having been her property. It was found in Fiddler Dick's watch fob.

" SLOUGH, 11.51 a.m.—Several of the suspected persons who came by the various down trains are lurking about Slough, uttering bitter invectives against the telegraph. Not one of those cautioned has ventured to proceed to the Montem."

In the following year the part that the electric telegraph took in bringing a murderer to justice riveted public attention on the practical utility of the new means of communication. A man named Tawell who had committed a murder at Salt Hill, boarded a train at Slough for London, and no doubt considered himself safe from capture. But the railway telegraph flashed a description of him to Paddington, from where he was followed to the City of London and arrested. After this the public, who dearly love anything connected with a murder, flocked to see the new apparatus at work, cheerfully paying their shillings for the privilege of doing so.

CHAPTER THE THIRD

INTO THE FAR WEST

THOUGH the Great Western Railway, as originally constituted, ended at Bristol, it was destined to extend ultimately as far westwards as a railway could be carried with advantage. The important town of Exeter, the famous harbour of Plymouth, and the mineral resources of Cornwall, lured the rails to Penzance in stages. It was obviously to the interests of the Great Western to encourage the extension of the broad gauge into Devon and Cornwall, and thereby increase the traffic over its own tracks while rendering more difficult the invasion of those counties by any narrow-gauge rival.

We find, therefore, the Great Western Railway associating itself successively with the Bristol and Exeter Railway; the South Devon Railway, extending from Exeter to Plymouth; the Cornwall Railway, linking Plymouth with Truro and throwing off a branch to Falmouth; and the West Cornwall Railway, which runs from Truro to Penzance. Brunel was engineer to all these undertakings in turn.

The Bristol and Exeter Railway, 75 miles long, received its charter in 1836. The first half of the route, from Bristol to Taunton, is practically level, offering no particular engineering difficulties; and actually was opened for traffic on June 14, 1841. So that, on the completion of the Great Western in August, passengers could proceed considerably further west than Bristol.

The Taunton-Exeter section is in marked contrast with the other, for it crosses the high ground in the eastern part of Devonshire. From Taunton to Whiteball the rails rise steadily for 12 miles, the climb culminating in a stiff gradient of 1 in 85, and the Whiteball Tunnel, five furlongs in length. The track then falls, with rises here and there, to Exeter.

The railway was opened throughout in 1844, and under an agreement was operated by the Great Western Railway till 1849. From that time onward it was independent, though working in combination with the Great Western, with which it finally amalgamated in 1876. During the initial period, on September 2, 1844, the first public excursion train was run by the Great Western, from London to Exeter. The return fares were 48s. and 31s., first and second class respectively. Five hundred persons went from Paddington, and as many from other stations.

THE SOUTH DEVON RAILWAY

As long ago as the closing years of the eighteenth century the attractions of Devonshire as a popular holiday ground had created considerable traffic on the Exeter Road. Early in the " railway era " Devonians began to demand the conveniences of railway travel. Brunel was called upon, while still busy with the London-Bristol line, to establish a route from Exeter to Plymouth.

Brunel decided to follow the right bank of the Exe to Starcross, and then the coastline past Dawlish to

Teignmouth. Beyond that town the track would run along
the left bank of the river Teign, and cross it just before reaching Newton Abbot. Up to this point there would be hardly

" Cornish Riviera Express " running between Dawlish
and Teignmouth,

any gradients worth mentioning. But beyond it, in order
to take a reasonably direct line to Plymouth, it was necessary
to cross difficult country, including the southern skirts of
Dartmoor. Between Newton Abbot and Totnes a crest
has to be passed, with a tunnel (Dainton) at the summit.
The gradients on both sides are extremely severe, ranging
for nearly a third of the distance between 1 in 57 and 1 in 36.
Westward of Totnes there is another stiff climb on to high
ground, in traversing which many lofty viaducts were
needed to cross the deep valleys which run northwards into

42

Dartmoor. Between Hemerdon and Plympton the rails fall 273 feet in two miles, on a gradient of 1 in 43. The course is then level for a short distance, and after a further sharp climb descends into Plymouth, nearly 52 miles from Exeter.

Speaking generally, the railway was difficult to construct throughout, as the level part of it by the water's edge had to be interposed between the sea and the cliffs. In fact, some delay was caused in obtaining an Act by the Admiralty instituting inquiries into the possibility of following the shore between Starcross and Dawlish. In 1844, however, the railway was authorised. The Great Western subscribed £150,000 and had four directors on the Board.

Work along the bank of the Exe was hampered by abnormally low tides, which prevented boats landing the necessary materials. Between Dawlish and Teignmouth it was necessary to protect the railway by a massive sea wall, repeatedly damaged by violent storms. The hilly portion of the line presented difficulties in operation and Brunel's idea was to concentrate the rise and fall into four inclines which could be worked by auxiliary power. In other parts of the country ropes and stationary engines had been used, but this method was obviously not suited to fast passenger traffic, and eventually Brunel advised the Directors to embark upon an experiment which, whatever its intrinsic merits, at least furnished a very interesting chapter in the history of locomotion.

THE ATMOSPHERIC SYSTEM

Some time before this he had been attracted to the Atmospheric System patented by Messrs. Clegg and

Samuda, and tried on experimental tracks at Wormwood Scrubbs, Croydon, and Dalkey (Ireland). Under this system a cast-iron pipeline, about 20 inches in internal diameter,* was laid between the rails. The pipes had a continuous longitudinal slot along the upper side, to enable an arm or coulter connecting an internal piston with the vehicles to be moved to travel along it. This slot was closed by a continuous leather flap, hinged at one edge. The piston was attached to the forward end of a long frame, the arm to the rear end. An arrangement of wheels on the frame pushed up the flap in advance of the arm. On air being exhausted from one end of the pipe, the piston

Section of Pipe Used for the Atmospheric System.

was driven in that direction by atmospheric pressure, hauling the attached vehicle or vehicles with it.

The Atmospheric System aroused great interest among engineers, but it was roundly condemned by Robert Stephenson as being uneconomical on steep gradients. Brunel, however, held the opposite opinion and

* *A length of one of the pipes used on the South Devon Railway may be seen in the General Offices at Paddington Station.*

recommended the use of the system over the whole length of the South Devon Railway, the needs of which it appeared to meet in an admirable manner. He considered that a single line operated by the Atmospheric System would carry as much traffic as a double line worked with locomotives, on account of the greater speed attainable, and that by adopting it a saving in first outlay of £67,000 could be effected, besides an annual saving of £8,000 in running costs.

Altogether, Brunel made out so good a case for the System that the Directors accepted his advice, and measures were at once put in hand for equipping the Exeter-Newton Abbot section.

When, in May, 1846, the line was opened to Teignmouth, the atmospheric plant was not ready and locomotives had to be used, as people showed impatience at the delays. The passage of trains interfered with completing the equipment, and the first trial run under atmospheric power did not take place until February of the next year. The Chairman of the Company reported to the shareholders that a speed of 70 miles an hour had been attained with light trains, and 33 miles per hour with a 100-ton train. Some troubles that developed deferred the public running of trains to Newton Abbot until November, 1847, and another two months passed before locomotives were almost entirely superseded.

The pipe line was equipped with pumping stations at intervals of about three miles. When a train was due, the engines exhausted the air, each ceasing to pump as soon as the train had passed. Owing to the lack of telegraphic equipment, preliminary pumping often lasted an unnecessarily long time, when a train happened to be late.

Atmospheric System Pumping Station at Exeter.

But on the whole the system worked well enough for a while, and at the end of February out of 884 trains moved, 790 had gained, or kept to, time. The passengers on their part were pleased by the smooth motion, the freedom from dirt and smoke, and the high speed attained, which on one occasion reached 64 miles an hour on the level.

But defects soon made themselves apparent. The cupped leathers used to render the piston air-tight were quickly destroyed by contact with the inlet and outlet valves at the ends of the pipe sections at stations. A much more serious trouble arose in regard to the longitudinal leather valve, upon the air-tightness of which the whole success of the system depended. Under the influence of heat, wet, and frost, the leather quickly deteriorated, and became stiff and rotten in spite of the application of oil and soap. The tannin in the leather reacted on the iron with which the valve made contact, producing further deterioration, and rendering the material tender and easily damaged by the piston arm. Leakage of air ran the cost of haulage up to nearly three times what it would have been with

also RATS ATE THE 46 LEATHER

locomotive power : and on occasions brought trains to a standstill. Brunel, after making a thorough investigation, found himself compelled to advocate scrapping the Atmospheric System and reverting to locomotives. As the accounts for the half-year ending June 30, 1848, showed a working loss of about £2,500, the Directors announced that on and after September 9 the Atmospheric System would be abandoned.

The failure was a great blow to Brunel's reputation ; and it hit him very hard financially also, as he had risked a large amount of his own money in the apparatus. The Company lost, so it was reported, from £300,000 to £400,000, and was left with a single line including very heavy gradients that taxed locomotives severely.

In 1848 the line was opened to Plymouth, and the same year the Torquay branch was completed. Thirty years later the South Devon Railway was taken over by the Great Western Railway.

THE CORNWALL RAILWAY

An Act authorising the construction of a railway from Plymouth to Truro and Falmouth was obtained in 1846, but the generally prevailing " tightness " of money during the slump following the Railway Mania prevented any considerable constructional work being done for some years. A serious start was not, in fact, made till 1853, and in the meantime it had become necessary to obtain a supplementary Act extending the time of construction till 1860. The railway runs through very broken country and a notable feature of it is the great number of viaducts—there are 34 of these between Plymouth and Truro, totalling over 4 miles in length—required to carry the rails across the many valleys with which the country is seamed.

Viaducts were adopted in place of embankments on account of the scarcity of filling material ; and the imperative need for economy induced Brunel to employ a large amount of timber in their construction. To facilitate repairs, a more or less standardised design was used. The viaducts had masonry piers, 66 feet apart, centre to centre, carried up to 35 feet below rail level. From the top of each pier four sets of four great beams radiated upwards fanwise, to carry three longitudinal lines of stout horizontal beams, two deep. These were in turn covered by transverse beams

Penryn Viaduct.

forming a decking 6 inches thick. Lateral stability was ensured by diagonal braces and tie bars between the sets of struts.

48

St. Pinnock Viaduct

The loftiest viaduct on the railway is that at St. Pinnock, the rails here being 153 feet above the ground.

The structures, which were found also on the South Devon and West Cornwall Railways, are unique in this country, and the nearest approach to the trestle bridges of America. On account of the need for periodical repair, all of those on the main line have been reconstructed, brick or granite arches and steel girders taking the place of timber-work ; but on the Falmouth branch a few of the old viaducts are still in service, though being replaced rapidly by embankments.

THE ROYAL ALBERT BRIDGE

Interesting as the viaducts are, they are comparatively insignificant beside Brunel's last and greatest feat of railway engineering, the Royal Albert Bridge spanning the river Tamar at Saltash. The river is 1,100 feet wide, and as the Admiralty insisted that any structure thrown across it should give a headway of at least 100 feet for vessels passing to and from the important naval base at Devonport, and not obstruct the fairway unduly, Brunel at first projected a single main span 850 feet long. Such a span had never yet been attempted, and eventually he drew out plans for a bridge with two main spans of 455 feet each, and long approach viaducts. The Britannia Bridge built by Robert Stephenson across the Menai Straits, and opened in 1850, had two spans of even greater length—460 feet—but whereas Stephenson had the advantage of a rock in mid channel for a central pier, Brunel was confronted by water 70 feet deep, with a thick layer of mud below it, overlying the rock on which the pier must be founded.

After exploring the bed of the river with the aid of a vertical cylinder 85 feet high and 6 feet in diameter, and

Saltash Bridge.

having satisfied himself that a pier could be built on the rock, Brunel completed his plans for constructing it. On the shore close by was assembled a huge cylinder, 35 in diameter at the bottom and 95 feet long. Twenty feet from the bottom a transverse diaphragm formed the roof of what would in effect be a diving bell; and from the centre of this to the top rose a central shaft 10 feet across, with a smaller working shaft and air-lock inside it. The space under the diaphragm was divided into a central circular space and a number of radial spaces between it and the outside of the cylinder, any one of which could be used separately as a diving bell.

The cylinder was sunk vertically on its site on June, 1854, and gradually allowed to settle on to the rock below. By February, 1855, it was in its final position, and the work of filling the iterior with masonry was begun. Springs in the rock gave a good deal of trouble but were eventually stopped out with concrete. When the masonry reached the roof of the diving-bell portion, the roof was removed, also the interior cylinder, and the masons completed the pier under the protection of the outer cylinder, the top part of which was unbolted and removed as soon as the cap of the pier had been finished.

Saltash Bridge under Construction.

On the pier were erected four octagonal cast-iron columns of the same height as the two masonry piers at the ends of the approach viaducts.

Meanwhile the two great trusses for the main spans were being put together on the river bank. Each of these consisted of an arch-shaped oval tube $16\frac{3}{4}$ feet broad and $12\frac{1}{4}$ feet high, having its ends connected by two massive chains of link plates. It has been described as " a combination of an arch and a suspension bridge, half the weight being placed on the one and half on the other, the outward thrust of the arch on the abutments being counter-balanced by the inward drag of the chains." Arch and chains are connected at eleven points by upright standards braced by diagonal bars and carrying the roadway girders. At the centre a truss is 56 feet deep. Its weight is 1,060 tons.

The raising of these ponderous structures into position, 110 feet above the water, was a formidable task, but Brunel had assisted Stephenson in raising the great tubes of the Britannia Bridge and used again the method which had proved so successful in that case. Each truss was lifted from its berth by large iron pontoons, and floated into position between the piers. After a thorough rehearsal, so that no mistake should be made, the first truss was moved from the shore on September 1, 1857, and, under the direction of Brunel himself, drawn into place by hawsers. Water having been admitted into the pontoons, the truss settled on to the piers and the pontoons were floated away. The occasion was made the excuse for general holiday in the neighbourhood, and between thirty and forty thousand people assembled to watch the operation.

The truss was raised by hydraulic jacks placed under-neath, in lifts of three feet, the masonry of the land pier being built up as the truss rose. To prevent any possi-bility of a fall, the rams of the jacks had large nuts on them, which were screwed down hard as the rams left the presses.

The Prince Consort, in whose honour it was named, opened the Bridge on May 3, 1859. Brunel was away on the Continent for his health, and the only view he had of his completed bridge was from a truck on which the great

Saltash Bridge.

engineer, then a very sick man, was slowly drawn across it. He died on September 15, and the Great Western lost the most distinguished of the men ever associated with it. He lies in Kensal Green Cemetery, close to the railway which he had served so long and faithfully.

The opening of the Saltash Bridge was also the opening of the Cornwall Railway. The way was now clear for a continuous run from London to Truro. In 1861 the Great Western Railway leased the line, and in 1889 the lease was cancelled in favour of amalgamation.

The Falmouth branch—11¾ miles long· came into use in August, 1863 ; the next year it was extended to the

Falmouth Harbour in 1866.

new docks then in course of construction. By 1866 a tidal harbour, with an area of 42 acres, had been formed by building a straight and an L-shaped breakwater. The Dock Company then ran short of money, and development work had to stop until funds had been provided by the

Public Works Loan Board for the completion of the docks. With this help fine facilities were provided for dry-docking and repair work, and these in turn brought a prosperity that enabled the loan to be paid off in 1915. The harbour which practically owes its existence to the Great Western Railway, became very important during the war as a naval base, owing to its geographical position. Since the war the Docks have been acquired by a very powerful group of shipowners and ship repairers, and have been considerably enlarged.

THE WEST CORNWALL RAILWAY

This last link in the present Great Western chain was developed out of a narrow-gauge railway opened in 1841 between Redruth, the Cornish mining centre, and Hayle, on St. Ives Bay, to transport minerals to the seaboard and bring up Welsh coal to the mines. The original track included two inclines, operated by ropes, but these were subsequently abolished.

In 1850 an Act was obtained for extending the Redruth-Hayle line westwards to Penzance and eastwards to Truro under the title of the West Cornwall Railway. The western extension was completed first (1851), and in the next year trains were running from Truro to Penzance, without, of course, having any connection with the Broad Gauge system, as the Cornwall Railway had not yet been constructed. The line was hardly a success financially; in fact, it had got into very low water by the time the Cornwall Railway was opened. An agreement was, therefore, made with the other Broad Gauge companies, and a third rail was laid down to enable broad gauge stock to run right through to Penzance. The first broad gauge train reached that town in 1860, and the way to the far west of England was clear from London to Mounts Bay.

Maps are apt to convey rather wrong impressions of distances, and it may come as a surprise to some readers to learn that, if a circle be described with London as centre and London-Penzance as radius, it will pass through Carlisle, close to the Scottish Border.

THE CLASH BETWEEN THE GAUGES

IMULTANEOUSLY with the advance of the Broad Gauge into the far south-west it was spreading northwards into the Midlands, southwards across the territory occupied or to be occupied by the narrow-gauge London and South Western Railway, and westward into Wales. The decade 1843 to 1853 witnessed a great extension of its mileage, with the backing of the Great Western Railway, which acquired one after another of the originally more or less independent broad-gauge enterprises. It was only natural that the first, largest and most powerful of the broad-gauge companies should swallow the smaller concerns, since amalgamation brought mutual benefits with it.

Thus, in 1843, the Great Western absorbed the line running from Swindon to Gloucester and Cheltenham ; in 1844 that connecting Didcot with Oxford ; in 1845 the Berks and Hants railways from Reading to Hungerford, and from Reading to Basingstoke. To carry the war into " enemy "—otherwise narrow-gauge—country, Bills were introduced and passed in 1845 authorising the Oxford and Rugby, the Wilts, Somerset and Weymouth (Bath and Chippenham to Trowbridge, Yeovil and Weymouth), the Oxford, Worcester and Wolverhampton, and

Difficulties incidental to a break of Gauge.

the South Wales (Gloucester to New Milford) broad-gauge railways. These subsequently became part of the Great Western system—the two first mentioned in 1850 and 1851 respectively, and the remaining two in 1863.

The narrow-gauge party on their side had not been idle, for in 1840 the Birmingham to Gloucester railway was opened, thus reaching Gloucester well ahead of the broad gauge. An independent broad-gauge railway between Bristol and Gloucester was completed in 1844, but in order to approach the latter town it had to make a working agreement with the Great Western Railway whereby it was allowed running powers over nine miles of the Swindon-Gloucester track.

Gloucester, then, was the first place at which the two rival gauges came into conflict. The Midland Railway, an amalgamation formed, in 1844, of the North Midland, Midland Counties, and Birmingham and Rugby Junction systems, were very anxious to purchase both the Birmingham and Gloucester and the Bristol and Gloucester lines, as a conversion of the latter to narrow-gauge would give direct access from the Midlands to Bristol, the most important city—London excepted—on the broad-gauge system. The Great Western directors, on the other hand, felt the great inconvenience of a break of gauge at Gloucester, and were in the market also. The Midland Railway, however, made the higher bid and, almost before the Great Western directors realised it, had got possession of both railways. They were unable, owing to a contract for locomotive service, to convert the Gloucester to Bristol track till several years later, but their victory dealt a somewhat heavy blow to the broad-gauge cause.

Paul Gooch

GREAT WESTERN RAILWAY

Locomotive Report for week ending Thursday 29 November —— 1838.

A Locomotive Report (or Expenses Sheet) for week ending November 29th, 1838.

THE CLASH BETWEEN THE GAUGES

It was inevitable that a clash should occur sooner or later between the gauges. As has been mentioned already, even among the Great Western shareholders there was a narrow gauge party. In 1845 the mileage of existing broad-gauge tracks totalled 274 as against 1,901 miles of narrow-gauge, and the champions of the latter argued with a good deal of reason that, as one or the other would have to give way to prevent future complications, the later-comer, with far less track to be altered, was indicated as the one to stand down. The confusion caused by transhipment of goods at Gloucester afforded a good " platform " for a campaign against the broad gauge, while passengers who had experienced the delays and inconveniences of changing trains naturally felt that something must be done.

A ROYAL COMMISSION APPOINTED

Eventually, a Royal Commission was appointed in July, 1845, to investigate the whole question and make suggestions for improving matters in the future. The railway companies were at once requested to furnish information as to the relative merits of the broad and the narrow gauge, delays caused by transhipment, and cost and particulars of engineering work, locomotives, and other rolling stock. For nearly five months the Commissioners took the evidence of 48 witnesses. Of these, 35 favoured the narrow gauge, eight were for a gauge of from 5 to 6 feet, and the remaining five, including, of course, Brunel and Daniel Gooch, his Locomotive Superintendent, were wholeheartedly for the broad gauge.

Towards the close of the enquiry Gooch suggested that a practical method of testing the comparative merits of the two gauges would be to run trains of equal weight under the observation of the Commissioners, and to compare results. After some discussion it was agreed that trials should be made between London and Didcot (53 miles) and between York and Darlington (45 miles) on the broad and narrow gauge respectively. The Broad Gauge party were in favour of longer runs, but to this the other side would not consent.

On December 16, 1845, the Great Western led off with an express engine and a passenger train load of over 81 tons. The run to Didcot was made in 64 minutes and the return journey in $60\frac{1}{4}$ minutes. On the following day the performance was repeated with a 60-ton train, the times being $62\frac{1}{2}$ and 59 minutes for the down and up runs respectively. On the same date a 400-ton goods train travelled to Didcot and back at an average speed of 24 miles an hour.

The narrow-gauge runs, which took place on December 30 and the two succeeding days, showed up pretty badly, as the 80-ton train averaged only 44 miles, and the 400-ton goods train only 19 miles per hour. Moreover, to put the matter mildly, there seems to have been a regrettable absence of the " sporting " spirit among the narrow-gaugers.

At any rate the broad-gauge engines came out of the trials with flying colours, and their behaviour no doubt influenced the Report of the Commissioners. This credited the broad gauge with greater comfort and safety at high speeds, and with a capacity for higher speeds than the narrow. But, on the ground that general convenience in transport was of greater importance than high speed, the Commissioners recommended that the gauge of 4 ft. $8\frac{1}{2}$

inches should be used on all railways then under construction ; that no railway should be allowed to alter its
gauge without Parliamentary sanction ; and that, where
the two gauges met, the broad gauge should give way to
the narrow, or, alternatively, means should be adopted for
allowing narrow-gauge carriages to travel over broad-gauge
lines.

The Gauge Regulation Act of August, 1846, toned down
the recommendations somewhat, for it included a clause
that a gauge other than 4 ft. 8½ inches was to be used
only under special powers ; and it expressly allowed the
South Wales, Oxford and Rugby, and Oxford, Worcester and Wolverhampton Railways to be laid down as
broad-gauge tracks ; though, as a concession to the other
side, the last two had to add a third rail to give narrow-
gauge trains access to Oxford.

The Oxford and Rugby railway, which ran through Banbury and thence northwards to Fenny Compton, became
Great Western property in 1850. Already, in 1846, broad-
gauge lines had been sanctioned from Fenny Compton
to Birmingham, and thence to Wolverhampton, giving that
gauge access to the very heart of the Midlands. Moreover,
the Great Western obtained under the Act a lease of 999
years. In spite of the most strenuous efforts of the London
and North Western to obtain control of this intruder into
its preserves, the Great Western had broad-gauge trains
running into Birmingham by 1852, and a year later acquired
the railway. In 1853 the broad-gauge track from Oxford to
Wolverhampton, *via* Worcester, was open, and, though
owned by an independent company, gave the Great Western
a path to the North. Not content with reaching Birmingham

and Wolverhampton, the Great Western acquired, in 1854, the narrow-gauge Shrewsbury to Birmingham, and Shrewsbury to Chester railways, and so had an independent route to the borders of Lancashire. But, as Parliament prohibited the laying of a third rail for broad-gauge rolling stock on these tracks, passengers were for some years obliged to change trains at Oxford while travelling " Great Western " from London to the North.

From 1854 onwards it may be said that the Great Western's main expansion was confined to that part of England west of the London—Oxford—Birmingham—Chester line, and north of the main route to Cornwall ; and to Wales. The latter country is dealt with in the next chapter.

THE WAY TO WALES

THE Bill introduced into Parliament in 1844 to obtain powers for building a railway across South Wales specified a route starting from Stonehouse, on the Swindon-Gloucester railway, crossing the Severn where it makes a horseshoe bend opposite Newnham, then following the right bank of the Severn to Chepstow, and passing through or near Newport, Cardiff, Swansea, and Carmarthen, into Pembrokeshire, which it would traverse to Fishguard Bay, on the northern coast of that county. Fishguard had many years previously been recommended by the Admiralty as a very suitable alternative to Milford Haven for packets plying between England and Ireland; since one or the other would offer refuge from a gale blowing anywhere between north and south.

A bridge over the Severn was objected to as a hindrance to navigation, but powers for a railway westwards of Chepstow to Milford were granted. In 1845, however, a second Act gave facilities for extending the line northwards from Chepstow to Grange Court on the railway from Gloucester to Hereford *via* Ross. This extension completed a through route *via* Gloucester and Swindon to London, albeit a somewhat roundabout one, and provided an important outlet for the coal and iron of South Wales, besides quicker travelling to Southern Ireland. That the promoters of the Great Western Railway had extensions to Wales in mind is indicated by the Preamble to the Act of Incorporation of that railway, which includes the words :—" Also by improving the existing communications between the metropolis and the Western districts of England, the *South of Ireland and Wales*, etc."

CHEPSTOW BRIDGE

The Great Western obtained, in 1846, a lease in perpetuity of the line, and Brunel was appointed engineer.

Chepstow Bridge.

The chief engineering works that he had to carry out in connection with the railway were : bridges over the

Severn at Gloucester, over the Wye at Chepstow, and over the Usk near Newport ; the Landore viaduct, near Swansea, one third of a mile long ; and a tunnel of about the same length near the same town. Of these the Chepstow Bridge was by far the most difficult. At the point where it stands the left bank of the river rises to a height of 120 feet, whereas the right bank slopes gently downwards towards the water. Since a headway of 50 feet above high water had to be left for navigation, the bridge had to be approached at one end by a cutting in the cliffs and at the other by a high embankment. The space to be bridged was 600 feet wide, divided into a river span of 300 feet, and three land spans of 100 feet each. The southern end of the main span rests on large cast iron cylinders sunk by the pneumatic process, in the manner described already in connection with the Saltash Bridge. As the railway has a double track, a separate main truss was constructed for each line. A truss consisted of a horizontal tube, 9 feet in diameter, connected with the girder carrying the track by suspension chains and upright standards.

The first truss was assembled on the river bank, tested, and taken to pieces. The tube, with parts of the suspension chains attached to it, was then floated into the line of the bridge, and lifted into position by powerful tackles, when the other parts of the truss were added to it. The bridge was opened for one line on July 14, 1852, and the second truss completed soon afterwards. The structure, which cost £77,000, gave Brunel useful experience that he turned to account later, while building the much larger bridge at Saltash.

To cross the River Usk, Brunel constructed a timber viaduct having eleven spans of 40 to 52 feet and a main channel span of 100 feet. When the viaduct had almost reached completion it was partially destroyed by fire, through the ignition of the chemical used to preserve the timber. This disaster led Brunel to use three polygonal bow-string iron girders for the main spans in place of

Usk Bridge.

timber trusses. As the bridge carried two lines of way, three girders were needed, the centre one having twice the strength of the others, since it had double their load to bear. Brunel designed these girders quite " out of his own head," as they were the first of their kind. His skill in bridge design—already manifested at Maidenhead—was proved by the original girders surviving 70 years of use, at the end of which the locomotives passing over weighed at least twice as much as those employed when the bridge was opened. During the middle 'eighties the timber spans were replaced by iron girders on masonry piers ; and at the present time the work of doubling the viaduct to take four tracks—required by the enormous growth of traffic—is approaching completion.

Through shortage of money, the railway did not make very fast progress, and the first section, from Chepstow to Swansea, was not opened till 1850, and the Chepstow to Grange Court stretch till 1851. The completion of the Chepstow Bridge in the following year enabled trains to run through from London to South Wales. By this time it had been decided to abandon Fishguard as a terminus in favour of New Milford, on Milford Haven, which was reached in 1856.

Under the terms of the lease, the Great Western paid a rent of £46,000 per annum, and two-thirds of the net profit, to the South Wales Railway, besides providing locomotive power. But in 1861 a certain amount of friction developed between the two companies, and as the upshot of this the Great Western Railway absorbed the other. It now had three great main routes : one to Exeter ; a second to the Welsh coast ; and a third to Chester.

The circuitous route to Wales through Gloucester, and the heavy inclines between that town and Swindon in the neighbourhood of Stroud, brought into existence a short railway, called the Bristol and South Wales Union, between Bristol and New Passage on the left bank of the Severn, with a corresponding branch from Severn Junction on the South Wales Railway, to Portskewett, on the Monmouthshire side. The river is at this point about two miles wide. Long timber piers were built out into deep water, terminating in stairs and lifts giving communication with floating pontoons, alongside of which steamers could come at all times of tide. The railway and its connecting ferry were inaugurated in 1863, and absorbed by the Great Western five years later. Though it saved passengers a good deal of time while travelling between Wales and Western England, it offered no facilities for heavy goods traffic.

THE SEVERN TUNNEL

In 1863 it was decided to build a high-level bridge across the Severn near New Passage, and designs were got out for a bridge nearly $2\frac{1}{4}$ miles long which would give a clear headway to ships of 122 feet. Its cost was estimated at about £1,000,000. But the Directors ultimately decided to adopt a scheme put forward by Mr. Charles Richardson, who had built the stages for the ferry, for driving a tunnel under the river; and an Act for its construction was secured in 1872.

Severn Tunnel Entrance, English Side.

The Board thus committed itself to carrying through by far the most difficult of the many great engineering achievements to the credit of the Great Western Railway. Had the Directors been able to foresee the repeated setbacks that the enterprise was to encounter during the next fourteen years, the several occasions on which disaster threatened, and the great cost and anxiety involved, they might well have shrunk from attempting this greatest of all submarine tunnels.

From an engineering point of view it was extremely unfortunate that, near the Monmouthshire side, the river bed contains a gulley, named the " Shoots," with nearly vertical sides and a depth 50 feet greater than the average of the rest of the channel. In order to pass under the " Shoots " at a safe depth, it was necessary for the tunnel to descend 140 feet below the general level of the rails on each side of the river. To avoid gradients exceeding 1 in 100 the length of actual tunnel was fixed at $4\frac{1}{3}$ miles, with approach cuttings three-fifths of a mile and one mile long

Severn Tunnel Entrance, Welsh Side.

73

at the west and east ends respectively. The better to understand what this implies, one may imagine the tunnel transferred to London. A train approaching it would begin to head downwards at the Tower, enter darkness at the Bank of England, pass under Oxford Circus at a depth of 160 feet, regain daylight at Royal Oak station, and be on the surface again at Kensal New Town.

The inside dimensions fixed for the tunnel were :—
Height from invert, $24\frac{1}{2}$ feet ; width, 26 feet. It was designed to take two tracks ; and, a significant fact, these were to be of narrow gauge.

Trial borings showed that the tunnel would pass through rock for about half its length, and through clay, gravel and sand for the rest of the distance. As a precautionary measure it was resolved to sink a shaft on the western bank and run a trial heading under the " Shoots." This was commenced in December, 1874, and after 750 yards of heading had been driven successfully, the Directors decided to continue the bore from end to end before letting a contract. For some years things progressed favourably, but towards the end of 1879 the miners working uphill between the shaft and the Monmouthshire end struck what became notorious as the Great Spring. Fresh water poured into the works from a subterranean reservoir in such quantities that the men were fortunate in escaping with their lives. A few hours later the water stood 150 feet deep in the shafts.

A SERIES OF TROUBLES

This disastrous happening led the Directors to call upon their consulting engineer, Sir John Hawkshaw, to take charge of operations in conjunction with Mr. Richardson; which he agreed to do on condition that the contract for completing the tunnel was given to Mr. T. A. Walker, who had been associated with him during the construction of the Metropolitan and East London Railways. The Board's consent having been obtained, a contract between Mr. Walker and the Company was signed before the end of the year.

The contractor's first task was to block-off the Great Spring, by means of large shields, and then pump the workings dry. Great difficulties were caused by repeated breakdowns of the pumps, but eventually the water was got under control. The next step was to unwater the heading under the river. Divers were sent down to close a valve in the latter, and after several attempts the leader, Lambert, reached the valve and, as he thought, turned it off. The influx of water continued as before, however, and when at last the heading had been drained by sheer pumping, it was discovered that, owing to the stem of the valve having a *left*-handed thread on it, Lambert had opened a closed valve instead of closing an open one! The matter was soon put right, and the water that had collected easily got rid of, permitting a wall to be built to block out the Great Spring.

The great snowstorm in January of 1881, by cutting off communications and a supply of fuel, almost brought pumping to a standstill, and to avoid what would have been a disaster a great deal of valuable timber had to go into the pump engine furnaces. Not long afterwards salt water burst into the completed part of the tunnel at the Gloucester end, and a big leak in the river bed had to be plugged by dumping in bargeloads of clay. In the following year,

the Great Spring found its way into the workings again;
and another serious incident happened at the Monmouthshire end. One night in October there was an unusually

Tidal Wave in 1883.
Men in Boat Sawing the Timber.

high tide, which overflowed the sea wall and inundated the
flat, low-lying ground behind it. Water poured down a
shaft and would undoubtedly have drowned everybody in
the workings, which had no other outlet, but for the
desperate and successful efforts made by the men on the
surface to erect a rampart round the mouth of the shaft.

This was the last really serious occurrence, and by
August 1884 the tunnel had been completed eastwards
from under the " Shoots " to the Gloucestershire entrance,
and from the Monmouthshire entrance to near the Great
Spring. The last was taken in flank by a side tunnel, which
delivered the water to the pumps and enabled the men

to proceed with excavation. On October 17, 1884, the headings met, and in April, 1885, the brickwork lining of the tunnel had been completed. This lining, it may be mentioned, consumed 77 million bricks and 37,000 tons of Portland cement, and is 27 inches thick.

Though the Great Spring had thus been bricked out, it was by no means finished with. Hardly was the tunnel completed when the hydrostatic pressure of the water penned in behind the lining began to rise until it attained 57-lb. per square inch and caused leakage and serious displacement of bricks. Mr. Walker, who had just left for South Africa, was hurriedly recalled, and, on seeing what had happened, decided that the only remedy lay in allowing the water to enter the tunnel and pump it to the surface. Very powerful pumping stations were installed, and ever since the opening of the tunnel water has been raised continuously to the surface at the average rate of 20,000,000 gallons a day. Few travellers through the tunnel are aware that they pass close to fourteen huge pumps.

THE TUNNEL COMPLETED

On January 9, 1886, the first train—a coal train—ran through the tunnel. On December 1 of the same year the tunnel was opened for passenger traffic. It had cost, first and last, nearly £2,000,000—the price to be paid for bringing Cardiff an hour nearer London and Bristol, and for preparing the way for those great developments further west which are referred to in a later chapter.

The successful conclusion of this undertaking was a triumph for Sir John Hawkshaw, Mr. Richardson, Mr. Walker, their lieutenants, and the Board of the Great

Western Railway. Though by no means the longest tunnel in existence, that under the Severn taxed the resourcefulness of its engineers to a probably unparalleled extent.

For 38 years after its opening the tunnel was ventilated continuously by a steam-driven Guibal fan, 40 feet in diameter and 12 feet wide, situated at the top of a shaft near Sudbrook in Monmouthshire. The fan has now been replaced by one of considerably greater capacity— 800,000 cubic feet of air per minute—to meet the effects of the heavily increased traffic through the tunnel.

How the traffic has grown is indicated by the following figures, taken from the *Great Western Railway Magazine* :—

Year	No. of Freight Trains	No. of Wagons
1887	..	7,776	..	241,778
1897	..	15,703	..	501,398
1907	..	17,860	..	735,637
1917	..	23,122	..	1,085,892

The shortening by the tunnel of running distances between towns, as compared with the old route *via* Gloucester and Swindon is :—

London–Cardiff ..	..	..	15	miles.
Southampton–Cardiff	..	..	$61\frac{1}{2}$	,,
Weymouth–Cardiff	..	..	60	,,
Bristol–Cardiff ..	..	..	$95\frac{3}{4}$	,,
Exeter–Cardiff ..	..	..	$95\frac{3}{4}$	,,

From the figures it may be deduced whether or not the driving of the tunnel was worth while.

THE PASSING OF THE BROAD GAUGE

IT has been mentioned on an earlier page that the Oxford, Worcester and Wolverhampton Railway was constructed with " mixed " gauge tracks, allowing both narrow and broad-gauge rolling-stock to pass over them : and that the Great Western had purchased narrow-gauge lines running northwards to Chester. As coals and other goods carried from the north to Southampton had to be transhipped either at Wolverhampton or Oxford into broad-gauge trucks, and again at Basingstoke into narrow-gauge trucks, much inconvenience was caused : and to simplify matters a third rail for narrow-gauge stock was laid from Oxford, *via* Reading, to Basingstoke. This addition provided a through narrow-gauge route right down to the Channel ; with corresponding advantages.

In 1859 the " O.W. and W." obtained Parliamentary sanction to abandon the broad-gauge altogether and the third outer rail was accordingly removed. In 1860 this railway amalgamated with two other narrow-gauge companies, the Worcester to Hereford, and the Newport, Abergavenny and Hereford, to form the West Midland Railway. As control over the new combination would give the Great Western very valuable facilities, a lease was obtained in 1861, on condition that a narrow-gauge third rail should be laid from Reading to Paddington. In October, 1861, the first narrow-gauge train left the London terminus ; an epoch-making event which ought to have convinced the most hardened broad-gaugers that the doom of their gauge was approaching.

The mixing of the gauge along the main line to Swindon and thence to Gloucester followed more or less automatically, and eventually the third rail reached Exeter. In 1869 the G.W.R. ceased to run broad-gauge passenger trains between London and Birmingham and Wolverhampton.

It was only natural that the acquisition of narrow-gauge lines and the " mixing " of the gauge over previously broad-gauge sections should bring home to the management the great disadvantages of the mixed-gauge system. Among these were the high cost of maintaining engines and rolling stock of both gauges ; the heavy upkeep of a three-rail track, especially at complicated cross-over junctions ; the damage done to vehicles of different gauges when shunted together in sidings ; and the expenditure on transfer stations. In 1867 there were in existence about 1,500 miles of broad-gauge track and 700 locomotives for the same. The whole of the South Wales railway, the G.W. main line from Exeter to Truro, and various branch lines were still pure broad-gauge when, in 1869, it was decided to make a beginning with the " conversion " of the broad- to narrow-gauge—as distinct from " mixing." Conversion implied moving two rails closer together, so that only standard-gauge rolling stock could pass over the track.

THE PASSING OF THE BROAD GAUGE

THE FIRST CONVERSION

In order to gather data as to the cost and time involved by conversion, the 22½-mile stretch between Grange Court and Hereford, on the Hereford, Ross and Gloucester railway was taken in hand first in 1869. This line has many tunnels, steep gradients, and sharp curves, and was laid partly on the longitudinal and partly on the cross-sleeper system. The schedule provided for the work being completed in 7 days. During this time passengers were moved between Hereford and Grange Court by omnibuses brought down from London to ply on the old coach road, which thus regained for a short period some of the old-time importance taken from it by the railway.

About 300 platelayers were collected for the work. At the beginning of each day they were distributed along a four-mile stretch, a gang of 20 to every quarter-mile. By the end of the day the section of track had been converted, allowing a narrow-gauge train to collect the gangs and move them to the beginning of the next section, where a broad-gauge train, fitted with sleeping accommodation, kitchens, offices, smiths' shops, and stores, awaited them. The process was repeated day after day until Grange Court had been reached, and the balance of time in hand was devoted to a general overhaul of the track and sidings.

This conversion taught the engineers several valuable lessons. One was that everything possible should be done beforehand : such as the framing up of switches and crossings, the provision of " short " rails for curves, and the marking of transoms at the points where they were to be sawn through. Another, that the labour force must be sufficient to attack the whole line at once, and be subdivided

81

into gangs, each assigned to a definite section, which it would not quit till the work as a whole was finished. There must be no moving on from one place to another.

THE SOUTH WALES RAILWAY CONVERTED

The next conversion undertaken (in 1872) was that of the whole of the South Wales Railway from Gloucester to Milford Haven. This, reduced to single track, and including branches, totalled 500 miles. A huge working force of 5,000 men was collected and distributed along the railway, in depots 4 miles apart, each provided with living accommodation, tools, and stores. The preliminary work on the " up " line, selected for prior treatment, was completed while the track was being cleared of all broad-gauge trucks. Just before actual conversion all traffic stopped, excepting a limited passenger service on the down line.

The gangs then attacked the track, sawing off parts of the transoms, slewing the outside baulks and rail inwards, replacing the bolts, gauging the rails, and repacking the ballast. In five days the up line was reopened for, now, narrow-gauge traffic. After one day's rest, the gangs tackled the down line ; and before another week was out the conversion was complete, and a narrow-gauge service between London and Milford had begun.

From this time on one line after another was converted : the Wilts, Somerset and Weymouth ; the Brentford branch ; the Barnstaple branch ; and others : until the only solely broad-gauge stretches left were the Exeter to Truro section of the main line with its various branches to Launceston, Moretonhampstead, St. Ives, Torquay, Falmouth, and other places.

Converting the Gauge, May, 1892.

Conversion of Gauge.

THE PASSING OF THE BROAD GAUGE

THE FINAL CONVERSION

In April, 1892, a notice was posted stating that both main line and branches would be converted to narrow gauge on Saturday, May 21, and Sunday, May 22. To deal with 170 miles of track in two days was what may be called a " large order " ; but in this case the greatest possible expedition was essential owing to the fact that the Devon and Cornwall lines were for the most part single-track, and traffic on a very important route would therefore have to be suspended entirely during operations. To carry the conversion through punctually the most perfect organisation was needed.

Before the morning of the 21st every broad-gauge locomotive, carriage and truck, had to be east of Exeter for despatch to Swindon. All kinds of odds-and-ends on wheels, recalling the early days of railway history, were unearthed from their resting places to join the procession ; and by

Last Broad Gauge to Penzance leaving Paddington 10.15 a.m., 20th May, 1892.

midnight on the 20th every siding was empty, and from a railway point of view the railway was dead : except at Exeter and Plymouth, where a number of narrow-gauge engines and vehicles had been concentrated in readiness for immediate use after the conversion. Five thousand men were distributed along the line, in gangs, on the system that had been found to work so well for the South Wales conversion.

The last broad-gauge train left Paddington at 10.15 a.m. on the 20th—the " Flying Cornishman "—drawn by the famous " Great Britain." It was, for many people, a melancholy occasion, as so much of their lives had been associated with the broad gauge, and its passing seemed to herald a new era that might not bring improvement with it. All the way down the line people gathered to see the train pass. Many a coin was placed on the rails to be flattened by the wheels and be treasured as a memento of the old days.

The affection that the officials who had been longest on the staff felt for the broad gauge is illustrated by an anecdote related in the *Gentleman's Mazagine* : " The other day an ancient guard on this line was knocked down and run-over by an engine ; and though good enough medical attendance was at hand, had skill been of any use, the dying man wished to see ' the Company's ' doctor. This gentleman, a man much esteemed by all the employees, was accordingly sent for. ' I am glad you came to see me start, Doctor, (as I hope) by the up-train,' said the poor man. ' I am only sorry I can do nothing for you, my good fellow,' answered the other. ' I know that ; it is all over with me. But there ! I'm glad *it was not one of them narrow-gauge engines that did it !* ' "

Last Broad Gauge Train to the West, 20th May, 1892.

As the " Cornishman " traversed the double track west of Exeter, certificates were handed to the stationmasters stating that this was the last westward-bound train. The stationmasters, armed with their certificates, then gave written permission to the engineering staff to proceed with the work of altering the down track. The train was worked through to Penzance, and constituted the very last broad-gauge train to run—the up " Cornishman," which left Penzance at 9.10 p.m. An Inspector travelled on the train, which stopped at every station to Exeter, and, having satisfied himself that all trains to leave the junctions in advance had departed, he gave the stationmaster a printed notice addressed to the engineering department.

It ran as follows :—" This is to certify that the last broad-gauge train from Penzance has left this station, and the engineering department can now take possession of the line from the station in the rear up to this station for the purpose of converting the gauge."

At daylight on May 21, the gangs, which two days before had been brought in by special trains from all parts of the Great Western System, got to work. Each gang of 20 men was under a ganger ; to every three gangers was appointed a foreman, who in turn was responsible to the officials of the engineering staff. All the track being of Brunel's " longitudinal " pattern, the operations were precisely the same as those carried during the South Wales Railway conversion. The men worked with so good a will that by nightfall the gauge had been altered throughout, and the sleepers tied ; so that Sunday, May 22, was available for final packing and testing, while narrow-gauge loco-motives moved up and down to settle the track into place.

THE PASSING OF THE BROAD GAUGE

The Sunday night mail from Paddington to Penzance ran as usual, using the London and South Western track between Exeter and Plymouth ; and on the following day the usual service of trains was in operation.

The whole of the conversion occupied only 30 hours ; and was marred by no accident of any kind. A marvel of organisation, it wrote " finis " to the Broad Gauge with a flourish. The removal of the third rail along the " mixed " sections was done at leisure, but by the end of 1895 very little of the mixed track was left, and that only in sidings.

In preparation for the new order of things a large number of carriages and locomotives had been designed and constructed to be easily converted from broad to narrow gauge. The carriages were dealt with at Swindon, where the broad gauge bogies were lowered away from the bodies, and narrow-gauge bogies substituted. The arrangements had been so thoroughly worked out that a score of coaches underwent conversion in a single day. Convertible locomotives had their driving wheels moved inwards so as to be inside, instead of outside, the frames.

Broad Gauge Convertible Locomotive.

Of course, a great deal of the old rolling stock was useless for narrow-gauge service, and for many years after the conversion miles of sidings at Swindon were filled with broad-gauge locomotives and coaches awaiting their turn for breaking up. The cost of the scrapping or conversion of rolling stock ran into some £370,000, and this, added to the cost of altering the track, brought up the total expenditure on the change-over from broad to narrow gauge to nearly a million pounds sterling.

What the broad gauge cost the Great Western, first and last, allowing for the laying of a third rail, the extra width of embankments, cuttings, tunnels, and permanent way generally, and the expenses of transfer at points where a break of gauge occurred, has probably never been worked out—it is doubtful if it lends itself to anything like exact calculation. But it must represent an enormous sum.

CONVERSION INEVITABLE

Was the Broad Gauge a mistake ? This question has been asked many a thousand times. From one point of view it undoubtedly was, since unification of gauges had to come sooner or later, and such unification could not, for physical reasons, favour the 7-foot. It must be remembered, however, that at the time of its adoption, railways were in their infancy, and very few people foresaw that a railway map of England 100 years later would look like a small-mesh net : and that the railways composing it would be operating as practically one system. The idea of territorial working was then somewhat of an obsession, as there were such large vacant fields to occupy. Brunel, a man of wide vision in many ways, either did not realise how long a start the narrow gauge had obtained, or under-estimated the speed at which it would spread.

We may therefore agree—indeed, events have proved it—that a serious error was made when the broad-gauge received official sanction. But a further interesting question arises. Was the Broad Gauge a mistake *per se* ? Would it have been better for *all* the railways to have been broad-gauge ? There are doubtless many engineers who would plump for a more generous gauge than the British Standard, as it would enable larger and more powerful locomotives to be used and heavier loads hauled. A broad gauge makes for speed, while on the other hand it demands gentle curves. Brunel's gauge had at least one useful effect—that of setting, in an early stage of railroading, a high standard of speed, which stimulated narrow-gauge engineers to improve their locomotives to the utmost. The fast running of the Great Western trains in the 'forties was, however, due in large measure to the longitudinal system of sleepering, which, prior to the invention of the fishplate and the introduction of rails of heavy section, was ahead of the other methods employed. Could Brunel take a trip in the " 10.30 Limited," or watch the passage of the enormous loads hauled by American locomotives—running into several thousands of tons—his opinions would, no doubt, be considerably modified. And what would he say to the 1,500-ton trains moved over the 3 ft. 6 in. gauge of the South African railways, or to the 400-ton loads drawn over the 2 ft. 6 in.-gauge Barsi line in India ?

The great trouble with the standard gauge in this country has been that the Stephensons and other early champions of it did not allow sufficient clearances in tunnels and under bridges to permit the gauge to be worked with maximum efficiency. As a result British rolling stock has to be kept within much smaller limits, as regards width and height, than that used in other countries where the same gauge prevails. The weight-carrying capacity of a track is governed by its general qualities, including the strength of rails and structures, more or less independently of gauge. The American Pullman car is approximately 2 feet wider and 2 ft. 6 inches higher than our passenger stock; and the huge trucks used on American railways carry individual loads of up to 100 tons of coal, iron ore, grain, etc. But the gauge on which they run is the same as ours. The only British railways with clearances adequate to meet modern requirements are those laid out on the broad gauge by Brunel; and even there the extra space is useless, owing to rolling stock having to be able to move on other tracks with narrow-gauge clearances.

Brunel, who in the matter of shipbuilding was far ahead of his time, unfortunately came on the railway scene a decade or two too late. Had things been otherwise, our railways generally might have been laid out on a, perhaps, too wide gauge, with corresponding clearances. A contraction of gauge is, as we have seen, a straightforward, if expensive, measure. The extension of clearances, involving the reconstruction of bridges and tunnels, is, on account of the enormous outlay necessary, quite outside the scope of practical politics.

AFTER THE GAUGE CONVERSION

THE period of twenty-two years that intervened between the final conversion of gauge and the outbreak of the Great War is an interesting one in the history of the Great Western Railway.

It did not, indeed, witness any great extensions of mileage ; but on the other hand it was one of great activity. Gauge complications being definitely out of the way, the Company settled down to the task of developing this great system to the fullest and making it into one of the finest railway concerns in the world.

Speaking in general terms, this was a period of track improvements ; of widenings ; of constructing links needed to straighten-out the main routes ; of quickened services ; of providing more powerful locomotives and more comfortable and capacious passenger vehicles ; of making the public realise that there is a Cornish Riviera ; and last, but by no means least, of opening a shorter route to Southern Ireland. Side by side with the provision of greater facilities for travel we find much care being devoted to the organisation of improved goods train services ; important factors in which were fitting certain classes of goods rolling-stock with the vacuum brake, thereby enabling them to be run with safety at approximately passenger express speeds, and the construction of relief lines and extensive siding accommodation.

The final conversion of the gauge had in the first instance involved merely the shifting of the rails and their supports closer together : and the difficulty of the operation centred on the speed at which it had to be carried through. There remained the far more tedious, extensive, and expensive business of relaying the whole of the main line between Paddington and Penzance. The longitudinal timbers and bridge rails of over 500 miles of track had to be removed, and be replaced by some 1,200,000 cross sleepers and 67,200 tons of bull-headed rails, with their 47,000 tons of chairs, and 1,200 tons of bolts and fishplates.

In addition, a vast amount of labour was needed to alter a multitude of switches, sidings and branch lines.

At the end of 1893, 435 miles of longitudinal road existed between London and Penzance (branch lines excepted). Four years later this had disappeared almost entirely.

TRACK WIDENING

The great increase of goods traffic on the G.W.R. main line since the opening of the South Wales Railway had, even before the conversion of gauge, made it evident that two tracks were not sufficient for both fast and slow services. It was therefore decided to relieve the original double track between London and Didcot by means of duplicate lines which could be devoted to local passenger and goods service.

The widening was carried out during two periods. The first covers the years 1874 to 1882, when two new tracks were laid down in stages from Paddington to Taplow.

The rest of the line as far as Didcot was quadrupled between 1890 and 1896, under five contracts with four different contracting firms. A great deal of heavy work was involved, for all embankments, cuttings, the Wharncliffe Viaduct, and all bridges had to be widened to take the additional tracks. Maidenhead bridge was duplicated ; and some bridges had to be rebuilt entirely, and stations and yards reconstructed. Slough and Reading stations, which had but one platform for both up and down trains, were replaced by the present extensive stations having a platform for every main track, in addition to terminal bays. In fact, operations were on a scale comparable with that of the original construction of the line. While the engineers enjoyed the advantages of modern labour-saving appliances and the facilities given by the existing tracks, they had to deal with a number of obstructions which were not there in Brunel's time, or were the work of that engineer—such as old bridges requiring " mending with a new one." Some of these were removed by explosives. It is related that, when one of the old bridges in Sonning Cutting was blown up, the " tonite " did its work so thoroughly that not only was the bridge demolished, but the sides of the cutting slipped down, blocking both running roads and delaying the night mail train. At another point, between Pangbourne and Goring, an explosion was equally unsuccessful, for after the blast the bridge still held its own, and the operation had to be repeated.

An interesting little story is told of another bridge between Cholsey and Didcot. All the necessary arrangements for swinging the girders on a Sunday had been made, but the contractor's foreman declined to carry out the work on the ground that the weather was unfavourable. On the Monday, however, the girders were discovered to be in place. Owing to the weather clearing up, the foreman had called out his gang and completed the job, but without the usual precautions, such as the placing of flagmen, and without any of the Company's officials being present ! Possibly the Company took the view that " All's well that ends well."

At Purley, between Tilehurst and Pangbourne, some cedar trees were left between the main and relief lines, giving, no doubt, a very picturesque touch to the railway at this point. But alas ! they and a number of other trees had to be condemned as unsafe. One night, or early one morning, both lines were closed and travelling cranes came

Track between Ealing Broadway and West Ealing.

along with the necessary men and equipment : and a few hours later the doomed trees were lying on adjoining land.

The relief tracks are on the north side of the old " fast " tracks. Between Ealing Broadway and West Ealing stations this is plain for all to see. The two southern lines are separated from one another by the " ten-foot way " of the converted broad gauge, while the other two have between them only the ordinary six-foot way. It may be observed that the old tracks pass through stations without swerving, to permit high speed ; whereas the relief lines, intended for slow and stopping trains, in many cases deviate to negotiate bridges or approach platforms.

At the time of the final conversion of the gauge in 1892 there were about $12\frac{1}{2}$ miles of single track road between Exeter and Plymouth ; $52\frac{1}{2}$ miles between Plymouth and Truro ; and $27\frac{1}{2}$ miles between Truro and Penzance. Say, 93 miles in all. The first section was doubled throughout in 1894, with the exception of about $1\frac{1}{4}$ miles, which was dealt with when the Dawlish tunnels were widened in 1905. Most of the Plymouth-Truro section was double-tracked between 1894 and 1900 ; and the Truro-Penzance section was taken in hand in 1894 and given a second track in short lengths at a time—all but 5 miles, where the formation was left ready for rails. The doubling involved the replacement of Brunel's timber viaducts on the main line by more solid structures of stone and steel, wide enough to take two tracks instead of the original single road.

The effects of the doubling may be seen in the great improvement in train services to Devon and Cornwall and the consequent increase in the popularity of these counties as holiday resorts.

"Pendennis Castle."

AFTER THE GAUGE CONVERSION

HEAVIER LOCOMOTIVES

Consideration of space precludes any but a very brief reference to the heavier and more powerful locomotives built after the conversion to deal with heavier passenger and goods trains. The period under review was a busy one at Swindon, where the four-coupled express passenger " Duke," " Badminton," and " Atbara " classes were successively produced, to be followed, in 1902, by the six-coupled 4-6-0 class with 6ft. $8\frac{1}{2}$ in. driving wheels. In 1906 appeared the first six-coupled 4-cylinder engines

" The Great Bear."

for long-distance non-stop runs; and, two years later, the " Great Bear," the only " Pacific " (4-6-2) engine yet built for the Great Western Railway. This engine weighed 142 tons—the record for G.W.R. locomotives—and has recently been converted to resemble the " Castle " class, and re-named " Viscount Churchill." On the goods side, Swindon turned out some very powerful eight-coupled goods engines. Boiler pressures were increased from 160 to 225 lb. per square inch, and superheating the steam while passing from boiler to cylinders was adopted.

As having to do with locomotives, one may here mention the laying, in 1895, of water troughs between the rails at several points on the G.W.R., to enable engines to replenish their water supply while travelling at full speed.

Picking up Water whilst Running at Speed.

MOTOR OMNIBUS SERVICES

The map at the end of the book shows a number of routes, for the most part in Devon, Cornwall and Wales, indicated by dotted lines. These are the road routes of the motor-'buses which act as feeders to the railway and have proved a great convenience to the inhabitants of towns and villages remote from the railway, as also to tourists.

The first Great Western motor-'bus was put into service between Helston and The Lizard, on August 3, 1903, when the G.W.R. Road Transport Department came into existence with two low-powered motor vehicles. The Penzance-Newlyn route was opened soon afterwards; and ever since (the war years excepted) there has been a steady extension of the services. To-day 37 routes, operated by 123 motor omnibuses, are scheduled in England

and Wales. During 1924, about £120,000 was received in fares, 2,165,390 car-miles were run per week on the

The First Great Western Motor Bus, 1903.

average, and 4,186,537 passengers carried by these vehicles. The figures show plainly enough that the public has a great appreciation of these road extensions of the Great Western Railway.

A SERIES OF SHORT CUTS

There was a time when the initials " G.W.R." were facetiously interpreted as indicating the " Great Way Round." And at that period not entirely without some reason, as a glance at the map would show.

For instance, to reach Taunton from London, one travelled north-westwards from Reading to Didcot ; then more or less due west to Bristol, and finished with a wide sweep to the south. Again, even after the opening of the Severn Tunnel the route to South Wales was considerably roundabout between Swindon and the Tunnel. Similarly, to reach Birmingham, a pronounced detour *via* Didcot, Oxford and Banbury had to be made.

In short, each of the main routes of the G.W.R. contained a section which needed substitution by a straight by-pass, as it were. In addition, the way to Weymouth, *via* Swindon and Chippenham, left a good deal to be desired.

But things are different now, for a succession of cut-offs has shortened distances considerably on all the routes mentioned.

The first taken in hand was the Weymouth. By means of a new short line joining the Hungerford-Devizes-Bath line, at Patney and Chirton, with the old route *via* Chippenham and Trowbridge at Westbury, the Weymouth service was deflected southwards *via* Reading and Hungerford, and the journey between London and the port shortened by 14 miles. This new route was opened in 1901.

It served a second and even more important purpose as an essential link in a quicker route to the West of England, which required a further length of new track to join the Weymouth route, near Castle Cary, with Langport, on the Yeovil-Durston line, close to Athelney, famous by virtue of its historic connection with King Alfred. This connection was opened on June 9, 1906, so completing a southerly route between London and Taunton, *via* Reading and Westbury, 20 miles shorter than the old one *via* Swindon and Bristol. The " Cornish Riviera " express, which had been inaugurated on July 1, 1904, was transferred to the quicker route, cutting down the time of the world's longest daily non-stop run between Paddington and Plymouth from 4 hours 27 minutes to 4 hours 7 minutes—one minute being saved by each mile of shortening. The transference of the fast western traffic to the new route, besides reducing times, relieved the old main line on the north.

Before this short-cut was ready for use the "South Wales Direct" route had been opened (in July, 1903). From Wootton Bassett, a few miles west of Swindon, a new line was constructed fairly straight across country to Patchway, a few miles east of the Severn Tunnel on the old South Wales Union Railway, reducing the distance, as compared with the old Bristol route, by something over 10 miles. Newport is now reached in 2 hours 20 minutes, as against about 4 hours by the old route. The completion of the "Direct" line prepared the way for speeding-up communication with Ireland in conjunction with the shorter trans-channel service referred to elsewhere. The new route involved some heavy engineering work, including the Sodbury Tunnel, which is $2\frac{1}{2}$ miles long and comes seventh for length among British railway tunnels.

In shortening the route from London to Birmingham the Great Western Railway worked in co-operation with the Great Central Railway (now part of the London and North Eastern Group). The Great Western constructed a new line which branched off north-westwards from the old main line near Old Oak Common, about $3\frac{1}{2}$ miles from Paddington, and ran through Brentham, Perivale and Greenford to Northolt, where it joined a Great Central track. From Northholt to High Wycombe a new "joint" line was made through Ruislip, Denham, Gerrards Cross, and Beaconsfield, and a new length laid down from Wycombe through Risborough, Haddenham, Ashendon and Bicester to Aynho Junction, near Banbury, on the old

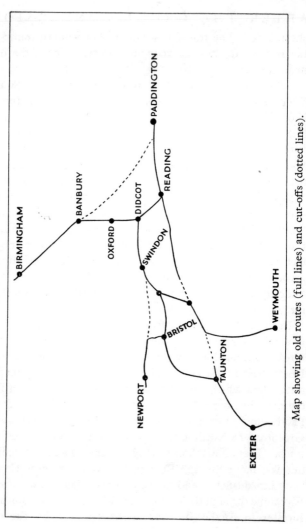

Map showing old routes (full lines) and cut-offs (dotted lines).

Oxford-Banbury line. The Ashendon-Aynho section
was, and is, purely Great Western, like the part between
Old Oak Common and Northholt : while the Northholt-
Ashendon central section continues to be owned jointly.
The new cut-off was opened as far as Wycombe on April 2,
1906, and throughout on July 1, 1910. As the distance
was reduced by nearly 20 miles, the expresses between
London and Birmingham were able to cut down their time
from 2 hours 20 minutes to 2 hours. The new cut-off
gives the shortest railway route to the capital city of the
Midlands, and, of course, also to Wolverhampton and
Shrewsbury, and rounds off the acquisitions of the G.W.R.
during the sixties.

The locations of the various links thus briefly described
are shown by the sketch map on p. 104, which will also
enable the reader to grasp their practical importance.

FISHGUARD HARBOUR

It has already been stated* that the western terminus of
the South Wales Railway was originally fixed at Fishguard
Bay, on the north coast of Pembrokeshire, but afterwards
transferred to New Milford. An important steamship
service between Milford and Waterford began in 1872, and
became to the Great Western what the Holyhead-Dublin
service was to the old London and North Western Railway.

But Waterford is a good many miles west of Carnsore
Point, the spot on Irish soil nearest to Wales; and
almost exactly fifty years after Brunel first mooted
Fishguard as the destination of his line interest in this
place revived.

* *On page* 67

Fishguard is famous in history as the scene of the last invasion by foreigners of British soil. During the years 1796-1805 Britons lived in terror of Napoleonic invasion, which was not finally laid until the victory at Trafalgar. The only practical attempt at invasion was made in February, 1797, when a French force, called " The Black Legion," landed and camped on the shores of Fishguard Bay. To oppose them, the first Baron Cawdor collected a troop of yeomanry and about three hundred men of the local militia ; and when these arrived on the scene they were joined by a large, but ill-armed, mob of miners and peasants, one section of which was headed by a militant clergyman and his double-barrelled fowling-piece.

Fortunately for the defence, the French force had no cannon and little discipline. The crews of the ships that transported it seem to have been a faint-hearted lot, for, on seeing an apparently formidable resistance being offered, they weighed anchor and abandoned their comrades to their fate. This desertion led to the French surrendering without a blow, leaving Lord Cawdor the bloodless victor of the " Three Days' War." The story is told of the surrender being due to the sudden appearance of a large number of Welsh women in red cloaks, mistaken by the enemy for the scarlet tunics of as many soldiers. Its authenticity is, however, too doubtful to be accepted, though women actually were among the ranks of the defenders.

The French selected their point of landing well, for Fishguard Bay is a fine sheet of water about 3 miles wide from East to West, protected on all sides but the north by cliffs ranging up to 300 feet in height ; while its waters are from 30 to 70 feet deep. Fishguard is but 54 miles from the Irish coast, as compared with about 100 miles between Milford and Waterford harbours ; and this fact brought into being, in 1893, a scheme under which, in 1898, the Great Western Railway became responsible for constructing a harbour at Fishguard, while the Great Southern and Western Railway of Ireland undertook a similar work at Rosslare, a few miles north of Carnsore Point. Both harbours were to be connected with the respective companies' systems by extension lines.

The point selected for the harbour at Fishguard is in the south-western corner of the Bay, where the sea then washed the foot of high cliffs. In order to make room for the necessary accommodation of a harbour, a huge notch had to be formed in the face of these cliffs, and the material removed used to build a breakwater and level up behind a long quay wall.

At that time the point on the railway nearest to Fishguard was Letterston, seven miles away, and from there all machinery, including the first locomotives, had to be hauled overland. To make an initial ledge in the cliffs, miners were lowered on ropes and blasting holes were drilled by hand. When space permitted, the work was taken up by powerful pneumatic drilling plant, and things went ahead more rapidly. In some places groups of holes 20 feet deep were charged and fired simultaneously by electricity. But, where conditions rendered it advisable, blasting was conducted on the wholesale scale adopted in large quarries. A heading driven at right angles to the face of the cliffs to a depth of 40 feet or more was extended right and left at the end to form a large T. From seven to ten tons of powder having been placed in the cross chambers, the

tunnel was securely filled up and the charge ignited. Some
of the big blasts detached upwards of 100,000 tons of rock
apiece. In the course of four years over two million tons
had been dislodged, and a level area of 27 acres formed,
partly in the rock and partly by dumping material behind a
quay wall built in the comparatively shallow water near the
shore, where there is a minimum depth of 20 feet. The
wall is 50 feet high, $19\frac{1}{2}$ feet thick at the bottom, and $13\frac{1}{2}$
feet thick at a point 3 feet below high water mark. To this
height it was constructed with concrete blocks made on the
site and weighing from 6 to 11 tons each; while above the
blocks mass concrete was used. The employment of

Irish Quay Extension, Fishguard Harbour.

reinforced concrete made it easy to form on the seaward
face a longitudinal gallery of half-arch section, into which

cattle are landed while passengers disembark at the higher level of the quay-top. A strong fencing runs along the outside, with gates in it at intervals ; while on the land side are subways leading to cattle pens near the passenger station.

The most impressive feature of the harbour is the great northern breakwater, which originally had a length of about 2,000 feet. A large part of the blasted rock was loaded into cars and dumped into the bay to build up a mound 300 feet wide at the base, 70 feet wide at the top, and about 70 feet high. Every foot run demanded some 650 tons of stone, so that the mole used about 1,500,000 tons in all. The seaward face, which is exposed to the full violence of gales from the north, had a protective facing of great boulders weighing up to 30 tons apiece, dropped into place by Titan cranes. The breakwater sheltered a water area of over a square mile in extent, easy of access and giving anchorage for a large number of ships, thus adding an important item to the list of British harbours of refuge.

When the Fishguard-Rosslare service was inaugurated on August 30, 1906, the quay space available had a total length of 1,120 feet, at which three large steamers could tie up simultaneously. On the cleared area stood a passenger station with 800-foot platforms, large waiting rooms, and all modern conveniences ; shunting yards ; and a power station. In the last is generated the energy for operating the electric traversing cranes on the quay and the haulage capstans which draw vehicles into position under the fixed cranes ; for lighting the harbour ; and for doing many other things which are best done electrically.

Since its opening the harbour has been improved very considerably. In the first place, the breakwater was lengthened by a further 900 feet, so that it now extends 3,000 feet into the water. Despite the size of the stones forming its outer face, the slope of the mole was altered by the action of waves, which gradually drew the stones down into a flatter gradient. To maintain height and thickness at the top, more stone had to be dumped periodically, and since this process would have continued until—as in the case of Plymouth breakwater—the rubble had attained the natural angle of repose and enormous quantities of material had been consumed, a contract was let in 1913 for securing permanence. Stones were dumped from barges along the

" Pell-mell " Blockwork at Fishguard.

foot of the outer face to form a kind of step below low-water mark, and above that the sea slope was armoured by dropping " pell-mell " or " random " concrete blocks, of 40 tons weight, more than 5,000 of which were needed for the work. The blocks are too massive to be displaced, and the waves expend their force on the openings between them. The top of the completed breakwater was paved and provided with a parapet ; and the outer end equipped with a lighthouse, the 5,000 candle-power lantern whereof is operated electrically from the shore end.

To increase the security of the anchorage, work on a breakwater running out from the shore on the further side of the harbour, almost at right angles to the main or northern breakwater, was begun in 1909. It has a length of 2,700 feet, and a round head whereon is erected a flashing light fed with gas from cylinders containing a whole year's supply. The burners are controlled by a sun-valve, which automatically turns the flames up and down at the beginning and end of the night.

The main quay has been lengthened by 700 feet to give room for two more steamers ; and a large area of foreshore by the eastern breakwater has been reclaimed, partly for a work-yard, and partly for a recreation ground.

The arrangements made at the port for dealing with the Southern Irish cattle trade are very complete. The ships carrying the cattle, sheep and pigs have trained cattlemen aboard to look after the animals. At Fishguard the cattle are driven into spacious pens, able to accommodate over 1,000 beasts, which serve both as a quarantine and inspection station, and a rest camp. Their second purpose is no doubt greatly appreciated after a stormy crossing, for cattle suffer in bad weather at least as much as do human beings. After a stay of ten hours during which an Inspector of the Board of Agriculture examines every animal very carefully, the cattle are transferred to special trains for despatch to the great distributing centres.

Fishguard harbour, which is particularly free from fogs, is kept dredged to give sufficient depth for large vessels at all states of the tide. An interesting feature is the meteorological station on the cliffs, fitted with weather-recording instruments and anemometers registering the direction and velocity of winds from hour to hour.

S.S. *St. Patrick.*

Some reference should be made to the fine ships used in the Fishguard-Rosslare service The *St. Andrew,* *St. Patrick,* and *St. David,* are 350 feet long and 41 feet in beam, and have a gross tonnage of 2,500. They belong to the awning deck type, and were built to class A1 at Lloyds', also to Board of Trade requirements as regards passenger steamers. For their size they are very high-powered, since their three turbines—each driving a separate propeller at 430 revolutions per minute—develop 9,500 horsepower between them. This accounts for their great speed of about 23 knots, which places them among the fastest ships in the world. Within three hours of casting off from one terminal quay a ship is alongside the quay on the further side of St. George's Channel. So it will be seen that these steamers maintain in their own element the high standard set by the G.W.R. on land.

THE GREAT WESTERN RAILWAY DURING THE WAR

IT was very fortunate that, at the outbreak of war, there was in existence an already well-worked-out scheme for making the best possible use of the British railway systems in a military sense. Under the Regulation of the Forces Act, 1871, the Government, by an Order in Council, took over the supreme control of all railways in the United Kingdom, so that the whole of the rolling stock and staff should serve as one complete unit.

A Railway Executive Committee, composed of railway General Managers, at once entered upon their arduous duties of operating the railways in accordance with instructions from the War Railway Council. The brain-centre of our railways was now a few rooms in which the Committee, assisted by but a dozen or two subordinates, issued orders to the heads of the various railways, who passed them on through the customary channels. While each railway retained its identity and staff, it now acted as but a branch of a much larger organisation.

The efficiency with which the schemes matured in peace time were carried into effect on the declaration of hostilities won world-wide admiration. At 11.45 p.m.,

THE G. W. R. DURING THE WAR

August 4, 1914, Britain entered the war officially. Fifteen minutes later the Government was in possession of the railways in readiness for the first day of mobilisation. Despite certain technical difficulties, such as differences in width of rolling-stock and type of automatic brake, the inadequacy of platform accommodation at some important centres, and the drain upon the personnel due to enlistment or the calling up of reservists, the despatch of the British Expeditionary Force was carried through with a celerity and absence of fuss and excitement which proved that, in railway matters at least, the British had nothing to learn from abroad. During the five days from August 15 to August 19, in addition to special local trains, 900 trains were loaded, despatched, and returned empty; the average being 360 trains a day employed for moving troops, and running into the ports at strictly timed 12-minute intervals. One port had to deal with 80 trains a day. The Fourth Division embarked on August 22-23, and on August 25 the docks were reopened for commercial purposes.

COAL TRAINS

The Great Western Railway played an exceedingly important part in military transportation from the first, and as the years passed it was more and more heavily taxed. The Great Western is the railway exit from the South Wales coal fields, which produces most of the steam coal used by the Fleet. In peace this was trucked straight from the mines in the Aberdare and Rhondda districts to the seaports and loaded on to colliers for movement by sea. But the scarcity of shipping and the perils of submarines and mines caused rail transport to replace coastwise carriage by sea. Consequently the Great Western was called upon to handle a great number of special coal trains from Pontypool Road to Warrington, where they were taken over by the London and North Western, and transferred by that

Coal Train of 100 Trucks.

railway to one of the Scottish railways for haulage to Grangemouth on the Forth. Here the coal was either transferred to colliers plying to the naval base at Scapa Flow; or stacked, to be drawn upon as required. The trains were worked to and from Warrington over three different routes. By the beginning of 1918 this Admiralty coal traffic had increased to a point where 79 specials, carrying 32,000 tons of coal, were needed every week. The number was subsequently advanced to 109 trains, and the load to 44,000 tons in the same period. During the war and up to the end of 1918 the quantity sent to Grangemouth totalled about 2,500,000 tons; while an equal tonnage was brought from the Welsh coalfields for dispatch to other destinations—Birkenhead, Devonport, Immingham, Glasgow, Burntisland, Southampton, London, Gosport, Hull,

Chatham, etc. " The fact that so great a traffic was run day by day, at practically time-table timings and for more than four years over some of the principal trunk lines of Wales, England, and Scotland, when immense volumes of other urgent war-traffic were being poured in upon these already heavily occupied lines, and when, also, the available resources of the railway companies in staff and engine power were steadily decreasing, constituted a remarkable achievement and one that might be regarded as establishing in itself the efficiency of the British railway system. Yet that efficiency becomes still more pronounced when one learns that the 13,630 war-period coal specials were run from South Wales to destination without any serious interruption on any one occasion. It was, indeed, having regard to all the circumstances and conditions of the time, a big undertaking ; but the British Fleet never once had to wait for its coal."*

GREAT WESTERN PORTS

The connection that the Great Western had with the great ports on the Bristol Channel—Avonmouth, Bristol, Newport, Cardiff, Barry, Swansea—meant a very great deal of haulage to and from these ports, to which, as a consequence of the submarine campaign, was diverted much of the traffic that otherwise would have gone to ports on the east coast. Enormous quantities of iron ore were landed at Newport Docks, which luckily had been greatly extended, and provided with the largest sea lock in the world, just prior to the war. The ore had to be distributed by the Great Western Railway to points *en route* to the great iron

* *"War Record of the Great Western Railway" by E. A. Pratt—p. 17.*

smelting districts. Nitrate of soda, and pitwood, cereals, fruit, and market produce, also came to Newport by the shipload, and required moving ; while from the port were sent all kinds of war supplies, including railway rolling stock.

Avonmouth was another very busy centre. Over 200,000 troops landed or embarked there ; and more than 130,000 truck loads of guns, ammunition, aircraft, and stores went out from the port to various fronts, especially to the Eastern fronts. Nearly 350,000 horses and mules were landed at Avonmouth from overseas for distribution. Altogether some three and a half million tons of goods passed through the port during the war.

Much the same story could be told of the other ports served by the Great Western. It must be remembered that, apart from goods coming in and going out, there was a huge movement of commodities from one part of the country to another by rail in place of by coasting steamers—steel, iron, stone, shells for filling, chemicals, china clay, and so on : and this all over and above the traffic connected with the ordinary needs of the community. In all, some 63,000 special freight trains were run over the Great Western system, carrying between 15,000,000 and 20,000,000 tons of goods.

As it now forms part of the Great Western group, the Midland and South Western Junction Railway may fitly be noticed here, since it was a most useful link between the North and the Channel ports. This line extends from Andoversford Junction, near Cheltenham, to Andover Junction, on the London and South Western Railway, *via* Cirencester, Swindon Town, Marlborough and Ludgershall. For nearly half its length—from Cirencester to

Marlborough—it has but one track. A branch line from Ludgershall connects the main line with the important military camp at Tidworth, on Salisbury Plain ; while its southern end is linked directly with Southampton by the (then) London and South Western Railway. It thus had a high strategical value, as is proved by the following summary* of its war-time traffic :—

Number of officers carried	..	181,683
Number of men carried	..	2,992,202
Number of horses carried	..	134,852
Tons of baggage carried	..	15,176
Special troop trains run	..	6,452
Ambulance trains run ..	..	1,488
Ammunition, truckloads run	..	9,021

At various points on the Great Western system upwards of 40 Government depots and munition works, and 230 privately-owned factories concerned with the making of war material, had to be provided with transport facilities. A very heavy task that fell on the Traffic Department was carrying the large number of people employed in these establishments to and from their work. Thus, the shell-filling factory at Hayes, in Middlesex, with its many thousands of employees, was served by anything up to 100 trains a day, and the number of passenger journeys made on these trains during the war period is estimated at 25,000,000. The same provision had to be made though on a smaller scale, at Avonmouth, Lando (South Wales), and Rotherwas (near Hereford.) Towards the end of the war the creation of the Mechanical Transport Depot at

---

* *Taken from the "Great Western Railway Magazine," Vol. XXXV., p. 497.*

Aerial View of Swindon Works.

Slough was begun; also that of the National Ship-building yard at Chepstow and Beachley. The completion of these projects involved the running of many special trains for workmen, in addition to the freight trains carrying materials.

In connection with munitions it may be mentioned that the Great Western Railway, in its Swindon Works, manufactured a huge quantity of war material, notably ambulance trains, gun carriages, ammunition wagons and other vehicles, shell forgings, fuses, copper driving bands, shell cartridge cases, and spare parts for locomotives and rolling stock in use in France and on other fronts. It should be stated that this very valuable contribution to the war equipment of the nation was made without any financial profit whatever accruing to the Company.

In addition to the 63,000 special freight trains (including coal trains), the Great Western Railway

6-in. Guns and Travelling Carriages made at Swindon Works.

ran, during the period of the war, over 37,000

special trains to carry naval and military passengers. Included in the last were 6,000 loaded ambulance trains, nearly half of which delivered patients at more than 40 Great Western Stations. Bristol was the destination of 395 trains, Paddington of 351 trains; and next to them, in order of number of trains, came Plymouth, Cardiff, Birmingham, Oxford, Reading, Birkenhead, Taplow and Paignton. The Company supplied four 11-coach ambulance trains for home service, and twelve 16-coach trains for use by British and American troops on the Continent. Some of these splendid trains were exhibited at Paddington and elsewhere before being put in service, and a considerable sum for charitable purposes was realised from the small fees charged to the public for the privilege of inspecting them. Members of the Great Western Railway staff who had qualified in ambulance work,

Ambulance Train.

but had been retained at home, showed much self-sacrifice in devoting their spare time to the unloading of the wounded and coming on duty during air raids, from which, fortunately, the Great Western Railway suffered no damage worth mentioning either in life or property.

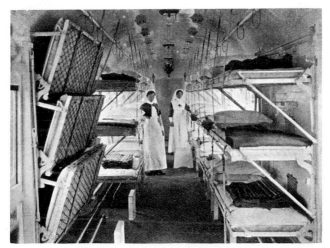

Interior of Ward Car of Ambulance Train.

THE G.W.R. WAR MEMORIAL

It need hardly be said that, when war was declared, the Great Western men were not backward in answering the call to arms. By the end of 1915 over 15,000 had joined the colours, and during the whole period nearly 25,500—about 32 per cent. of the pre-war staff—donned military uniform. The number of those who were killed or died of wounds was 2,524; and that of war honours gained over 600. On Armistice Day, 1922, the Great Western Railway war memorial in memory of the fallen was unveiled, in the presence of some 6,000 people, by the Rt. Hon. Viscount

The Great Western Railway War Memorial, Paddington Station.

Churchill, G.C.V.O., the Chairman of the Company. It stands on the principal main line departure platform (No. 1) under the central transept and immediately in front of the Royal waiting room. The following description of the War Memorial is from the *Great Western Railway Magazine*.

" The memorial is in the form of a wall treatment, and consists of a bronze figure of a soldier standing against a background of marble and granite. The soldier is dressed in the rough habiliments of war, with his great-coat loosely thrown over his shoulders. He has just opened a letter from home, which he is in the act of reading. On the great white background are engraved, at the sides, the badges of the Navy and the Air Force.

" A vellum Roll, on which are inscribed the names of the 2,524 men who gave their lives, is deposited beneath the figure, in a sealed casket made at Swindon works."

The memorial was designed and sculptured by Mr. C. S. Jagger, M.C., R.B.S., who served in the war from 1914 to 1918, as an infantry officer, was wounded twice, and received the Military Cross for bravery during the great German offensive of 1918. The architectural setting is from the designs of Mr. T. S. Tait, A.R.I.B.A.

Other war memorials to railwaymen were set up at Swindon and other places on the Great Western Railway system.

WOMEN EMPLOYEES

The depletion of the male staff by war service compelled the Great Western, like other railways, to substitute women and girls wherever possible. At the beginning of the war between 1,300 and 1,400 female employees were on the Company's rolls as clerks, typists, telegraphists, telephone operators, waitresses, charwomen, etc. By the end of the war the number had increased to over 6,000, more than half of the clerical work of the railway being done by women, and the greater part of ticket-collecting and carriage-cleaning. Nor did women shrink from tasks involving greater physical labour, for some hundreds of them handled baggage and trundled barrows as porters in Great Western stations.

THE G.W.R. STEAMERS AND THE WAR

In the very early days of the war the fast turbine vessels *St. Andrew*, *St. David*, and *St. Patrick*, used in the Fishguard-Rosslare service, were commandeered by the Admiralty to serve as hospital ships. The necessary alterations, which included the fitting of a large number of cots, and of lifts for moving patients from deck to deck, having been quickly made by the Company's marine factory staff at Fishguard, the ships took up their new duties between England and France. First and last they moved nearly 400,000 patients from Rouen, St. Nazaire, and other French ports, not without having their fair share of escapes from submarines and aircraft. At the conclusion of hostilities these vessels became troopships and assisted in the demobilisation of the British armies in France.

Of the ships that plied in the Weymouth-Channel Islands service the speedy *s.s. Roebuck* and *Reindeer* were taken over, together with the somewhat slower, but still fast, *Lynx* and *Gazelle*. Only the *Ibex* was left to carry on with her usual duties; and while engaged in these she had the good fortune to sink an enemy submarine. As she was steaming homewards one moonlight, misty night, the lookout sighted a submarine, which promptly fired a few shots. The *Ibex* replied so effectively that the submarine sank at

S.S. *Ibex.*

once. The captain and crew received from the Admiralty a sum of £500 in recognition of their services, and a plate was fixed in the saloon to commemorate the deed. The *Ibex* has since been sold, and two luxurious new turbine steamers, the *St. Julien* and the *St. Helier* placed in service on the Weymouth-Channel Islands route.

Her sister ships were sent to the Mediterranean and took part in the attack in the Dardanelles. The *Gazelle*, told off to help maintain the blockade of enemy ports, one day sighted a strange ship evidently trying to run the blockade, and gave chase. The *Gazelle*, being the faster ship, quickly overhauled the other, which was abandoned by her crew, who got clear in the ship's lifeboats. The ship turned out to be, by a curious coincidence, the ex-Great Western Railway steamer *Antelope*, sold out of the

S.S. St. Julien.

Weymouth service. Renamed the *Anthometus*, she was carrying a cargo of petrol and sulphur to the enemy when captured. A part of the *Gazelle's* crew took her into Suda Bay, and the French authorities used her for some time as a transport.

In spite of the reduction of its fleet, the Great Western Railway maintained its service between Ireland and England. Almost every night a ship crossed the St. George's Channel with a load of cattle, taking her chance of mines and submarines. A vast amount of live stock was thus landed at Fishguard during the war ; and it may safely be said that the food position in England would have been sensibly worse than it actually was had steamers not plied regularly to and fro.

THE LATEST PHASE

URING the Great War the British railways were operated, as we have seen, as national railways, though retaining their identity. For seven years control of the Railways of Great Britain was vested in the Railway Executive Committee. The Government did what they liked with the plant and equipment, which was not handed back to the owners until August 15, 1921. By that time, as the result of the temporary nationalisation, the condition of the railways was practically one of bankruptcy : expenditure having increased so much faster than revenue that for the period ending with the " restoration " it actually overtopped the receipts by £19,000,000.

The reason for this is not far to seek. Fares and rates had not kept pace with the enormous rise in the cost of materials and of wages. In fact, the Government made no increase in passenger fares till January, 1917, when they were put up 50 per cent. over pre-war level ; and this rise was not followed by another (of 25 per cent.) till August, 1920. Until January, 1920—that is, 15 months after the War had ended—railway rates and charges for goods and mineral traffic stood at the same figures as in 1914. Then they were suddenly stiffened by amounts ranging up to 115 per cent., and the business community,

now struggling to recover from the effects of the war, naturally was somewhat staggered by so great an increase coming
all at once. However, it was long overdue, as railway
transport was the only commodity that had not gone up
greatly in price during the war : and it had been rendered
inevitable by the much augmented wages bill that resulted
by Government concessions. To take the case of the
G.W.R., with which we are here primarily concerned.
Before the war its bill for salary and wages was, in round
figures, £6,000,000 per annum. At its post-war maximum
it reached just over £20,000,000—an increase of 233 per
cent.

In full settlement of their claims for arrears of maintenance and other damage to their property, the railways
together received £60,000,000, a sum which, considering
the conditions they had to face as regards cost of renewals
and wages, certainly did not err on the side of generosity.

RAILWAY GROUPING

A reduction of both fares and rates was as important
to the welfare of the community, as it was difficult to bring
about. The Minister of Transport, after much investigation, produced, in 1920, a scheme under which the railways
of Great Britain, some 120 in number, would be formed
into a few large groups, each controlled by a single management. In this way it was hoped to effect economies in
working which might render possible some reduction in
charges to the public.

A Bill was introduced into the House of Commons on
May 11, 1921, and this became law on August 19 following,
under the title of " The Railways Act, 1921." The Act

collected the railways of Great Britain and Northern Ireland into four large groups :—

The Great Western ;

The London and North Eastern ;

The London, Midland and Scottish ;

The Southern.

There remained outside the grouping only—

The Cheshire Lines ;

The Midland and Great Northern Joint Railway ;

The Somerset and Dorset Joint Railway ;

The Metropolitan Railway ;

The " Underground " Railways of London ; which between them have only about 1,300 miles of track (reduced to single) out of a total for the countries concerned of 55,000 ; and so amount to a very small percentage.

The " grouping " extinguished officially all the well-known names—" Great Northern," " Midland," " London and North Western," " North Eastern," " Caledonian," and so on, of the old big companies with one important exception. The " Great Western " remains " Great Western " amid the general change, and has the proud distinction of carrying on its title unimpaired.* Even it, we are told, had a somewhat narrow escape from being camouflaged under another name.

" A group " consisted of certain constituent companies —generally speaking, main-line companies—with their

---

* NOTE. *It is an interesting fact that the Great Western Railway was the first of the main lines of the country to receive, in 1835, the title by which it was afterwards known up to the time of grouping. Other dates : L. & S. W. (1839) ; Midland (1844) ; G. Northern, L. B. & S.C., L. & N. W. (1846) ; Lancashire & Yorkshire (1847) ; N. Eastern (1854) ; G. Eastern (1862).*

" subsidiary," or tributary, companies. The Great Western Group included as constituents the G.W.R., Cambrian, Cardiff, Barry, Rhymney, Taff Vale, and Alexandra

A SURVIVAL OF TITLE.

By courtesy of " South Wales News."

The Great Western : " Hooray ! Never even blew me cap off."

(Newport and South Wales) Docks and Railway Companies. With these were associated 26 small companies, nine of which had previously been worked by the G.W.R., four by the Cambrian, two by the Taff Vale, and one by the Barry Railway. The constituent companies had to evolve a scheme of amalgamation, and, when amalgamated, to submit schemes for absorbing the subsidiaries. Stockholders and shareholders in the other companies received

G.W.R. stocks or shares, the basis for allotment being the respective net revenues of 1913. Thus, a holder of £100 Taff Vale 3 per cent. Debenture Stock received £75 worth of 4 per cent. G.W.R. Debenture Stock; while the possessor of £100 Cambrian Railways " Ordinary " had to be content with about £2–15–6 in G.W.R. Ordinary Deferred Certificates.

The effect of the grouping on the G.W.'s mileage was to increase it by only 560 geographical miles, and by 3,365 miles of single track, sidings included, as the system already covered very thoroughly the country between the London-Penzance line on the south and the London-Birmingham-Chester route on the north-east. In fact, as regards England, the amalgamations altered the map of the G.W.R. very little, since the important constituent companies that entered the group are all in Wales. The capital of the Company was augmented by about £36,000,000; the number of employees by 18,000.

The Groups began to operate as such on the first day of 1923. Whether or not to mark the occasion in a significant and acceptable manner, passenger fares were reduced on the same date to 50 per cent. above pre-war rates.

Among the constituents of the Great Western Group are the Cambrian Railways and the Taff Vale Railway, to use their old names. As they are both of interest, we will take a glance at their history and " spheres."

THE CAMBRIAN RAILWAYS

This system sprawls like a distorted Y over northern and mid Wales. Its vertical leg extends northwards from

Brecon, past Builth Wells, Rhayader, and Llanidloes, to Moat Lane Junction. From this point the eastern arm of the Y runs through Newtown, Montgomery, Welshpool and Oswestry and Ellesmere, and at the last point forks again to termini at Wrexham and Whitchurch. The Western arm passes through Cemmes Road (to Dinas Mawddwy), Dovey Junction (to Aberystwyth and Devil's Bridge), along the north shore of the Dovey estuary to Aberdovey, and thence follows the coast northwards through Barmouth (branch to Dolgelley), Harlech, Portmadoc and Criccieth to the terminus at Pwllheli. Under the old regime the Great Western already had lines running from Shrewsbury to Welshpool; from Ruabon on the Shrewsbury-Chester line to Dolgelley; and from Carmarthen, *via* Lampeter, to Aberystwyth; so that the accession of the Cambrian was a natural rounding-off of routes. One can now make the circuit of four-fifths of Wales over Great Western track, thus: Newport-Hereford-Shrewsbury - Ruabon - Barmouth - Aberystwyth - Carmarthen - Swansea - Newport; that is, if the jointly-owned Hereford-Shrewsbury line be counted in as Great Western.

The " Cambrian," which has but one track for all except 27 of its 295 miles, and is thus the longest continuous single-track in England and Wales, was formed out of five railways constructed in the sixties. It traverses mountainous country and has several severe gradients, but only six tunnels. The most considerable engineering feature of the railway is the Barmouth viaduct, 800 yards long in 113 spans, crossing the estuary of the River Mawddach. This, for most of its length a wooden structure, includes a fine steel swing bridge at the northern end. From the viaduct a magnificent view of the estuary is obtained—a view that is worth going some way to see.

Barmouth Viaduct.

The very deep cutting at Talerddig, between Moat Lane and Dovey Junction, had to be made to open the road westwards. Many thousands of tons of rock were blasted out to form a deep trench along which the track runs at an elevation of 700 feet above sea-level. Another fine piece of rock work is to be found between Towyn and Barmouth, where the railway worms its way along a notch in the cliffs and one seems to be almost overhanging the sea far below.

The Cambrian was handicapped from the start by heavy cost of construction and the general sparseness of population in the country it runs through. It taps no great coal-fields nor other source of mineral wealth, granite excepted, and it serves no towns of first-class importance. It possesses a very valuable asset, however, in the beautiful scenery flanking its routes, and in the Welsh sea resorts of Cardigan Bay.

It may be doubted whether any other stretch of railway in Great Britain offers such splendid views of coast and hills as are commanded from the windows of a train travelling between Aberystwyth and Pwllheli. In spite of financial and other difficulties the Cambrian adopted a progressive policy for rendering its territory a favourite holiday ground and deserved the gratitude of the many tourists and other pleasure-seekers that used it year after year.

There were shakings of heads among the population served by the Cambrian Railways over the proposed amalgamation with the G.W.R., which already had some very useful holiday irons in the fire—to wit, South Wales, and the West of England—and, it was feared, might favour these at the expense of the resorts further north. That such fears were groundless has been proved by events. The great resources of the Group and the unity of control have brought many improvements to the Cambrian. Through trains now run from London to Aberystwyth and Pwllheli, and times have been cut down very appreciably. Restaurant cars are included in the summer trains to the coast. More trains figure in the schedules. Rail motor cars run on the Welsh tracks, which in places have been doubled. New signalling apparatus has been installed throughout ; bridges reconstructed ; crossing loops extended ; and last, but by no means least, some of the principal stations have been rendered much more comfortable for travellers. So far from losing by the amalgamation, the Cambrian system will, much quicker than it could have done if working alone, open up a new playground for the inhabitants of great English cities.

THE TAFF VALE RAILWAY

offers a very complete contrast to the Cambrian. It traverses a country which in the main is one of the most densely populated in Great Britain—that is, in the world—but can hardly be termed beautiful; it carries an enormous goods traffic; has from two to six tracks; and developed into one of the best paying of British railways.

The Taff Vale is the oldest of the Welsh public railways, and was the first to tap the vast mineral riches of South Wales. Towards the end of the eighteenth century the Welsh iron trade, centred in Merthyr Tydvil, had reached

a stage of great prosperity; and the need of improved means of transport led to the construction of the Glamorgan Canal, which connected Merthyr with the sea at Cardiff. By 1834, the zenith of its success, the canal carried over 110,000 tons of iron. It was to Abercynon, on the canal, that the famous Pennydarren Tramroad ran. This tramway was the scene, in 1804, of the first trial of a steam locomotive on rails. Richard Trevithick, the

Richard Trevithick.

inventor and constructor of the engine, made the experiment at his own expense, hauling a train of five wagons containing ten tons of iron and seventy persons for a distance of nine miles at a speed of five miles an hour. The tramway not being suited to the new method of haulage, steam traction was not a success and South Wales abandoned for the time an invention destined to be of immense importance to it.

Trevithick's 1804 Locomotive.

In order to smelt iron, large quantities of coke were needed and the ironmasters round Merthyr opened up the coal seams in the neighbourhood. There presently arose a demand from outside for the excellent Welsh coal, and the canal then proved unable to carry both coal and iron. Iron masters and coal-owners were soon up in arms against the delays in getting their goods to market, and determined that, as water transport appeared unequal to the task, some other means should be employed. The result was the formation, in 1835, of the Taff Vale Railway Company with a share capital of £250,000, to construct a line from Merthyr to Cardiff, paralleling the Canal. As might be expected, the Canal Company put up a very vigorous fight against the authorising Bill, and their opposition had eventually to be bought off by payment of a sum of £10,000. The Act obtained on June 21, 1836, had a length quite out of proportion to that of the railway to which it referred ; and among its 210 clauses was one limiting the speed of travel on the railway to 12 miles an hour, under a penalty of 40 shillings. This clause was handsomely transgressed by the first passenger train, which attained a maximum speed of 40 miles an hour ; and it soon had to be repealed.

The Company appointed Brunel as their engineer, and he built the railway with a narrow or standard-gauge track. When the work was well in hand, he decided that the gauge should be one of 7 feet, but things had gone too far for any alteration to be made, and the Taff Vale has therefore been a standard-gauge line from first to last. The first portion of the line was opened between Cardiff and Abercynon on October 8, 1840, the whole line being completed and opened in April, 1841, a few months before the completion of the G.W.R. throughout to Bristol.

In the early years of its history the Company had many difficulties to overcome, but in 1846 an agreement was come to between it and the Marquis of Bute, under which the Company obtained the sole right of shipping coal on the east side of the new West Bute Dock at Cardiff. As a *quid pro quo* the Company had to abandon a projected extension to Penarth and the construction of docks in the river Ely close by.

From the first the railway found plenty of work to do, for the facilities it offered led to a great development of the South Wales coalfields. Moving the heavy mineral traffic was assisted by the gradients, some of them heavy, running consistently the right way—that is, downhill—from the inland termini to the sea. Hardly was the line opened when the Great Western Railway completed a seven-year contract with the Dinas collieries for the delivery of 40,000 tons of coal per annum, all of which had to be carried by the Taff Vale tracks.

The demand for transport brought into being one extension after another, besides independent feeder lines, which were leased to or controlled by the Taff Vale. The Rhondda Valley was opened up by extensions from Pontypridd, and by a line carried from Abercynon to Aberdare. In 1889 a general amalgamation took place, bringing under one management the Taff Vale system as it was before it joined the G.W. group.

The main line after leaving Cardiff has six tracks for a short distance, and then four only to Pontypridd. Two tracks continue from this point to Merthyr; while up the Rhondda Valley the four tracks persist as far as Porth, where they diminish to three. The branches, of which there are 23, are for the most part double-track.

As early as 1855 the Taff Vale Railway began to experience difficulty in shipping all the coal it could carry, and looked about for some outlet additional to the Bute Docks. Accordingly it promoted in 1856 a separate Company for building a railway to Penarth and converting the estuary of the River Ely into a tidal harbour. Next year the Penarth Harbour, Dock and Railway Company was leased to the Taff Vale, in spite of the opposition of the trustees of the Marquis of Bute. The Penarth Dock, opened in 1861, has an area of 26 acres, and 7,580 feet of quays equipped with 18 hydraulic coaling tips. In this Dock over $4\frac{1}{2}$ million tons of coal have been loaded in a year—probably more than has been put aboard elsewhere in a dock of equal area.

General View, Penarth Dock.

THE LATEST PHASE

The Taff Vale, like other systems, has had its ups and downs, more or less coincident with those of the coal trade, but for many years it was one of the most profitable among British railways. This is hardly to be wondered at, in view of the heavy traffic, which has reached 11,000,000 passengers and 20,000,000 tons of freight in a year.

THE GREAT WESTERN RAILWAY DOCKS

One important effect of the railway grouping was to make the Great Western Railway the largest dock-owning company in the world. The Port of Cardiff ranks among the first ports in the world for the export of coal, and has long held a prominent position for the importation of general cargo. In addition to the Docks, to which reference has already been made, the Company acquired the extensive docks at Swansea, Newport, Barry, Penarth and Port Talbot. The water area of the Company's docks totals about 1,300 acres. The South Wales ports which came into the Great Western Group handle about 50,000,000 tons of goods per annum, three-quarters of which is coal, while the remainder comprises practically every other commodity exported from or imported by Great Britain. The chief exports are coal (easily first with about 35,000,000 tons); patent fuel, steel rails, plates, sleepers, and other forms of manufactured steel: petroleum and motor spirit. The imports embrace ores of all kinds; pig-iron; pitwood; timber; grain; flour; fruit; fish; vegetables; dairy produce; live cattle, sheep and pigs; frozen and chilled meat; and general merchandise.

The South Wales docks derive their importance from their vicinity to the great coal and iron centres of the

Principality, and from being the nearest large ports to the Midlands. Liner services ply at regular and frequent intervals between them and all the principal ports of the world.

Taken all together, the South Wales docks are equipped with 185 coal-shipping appliances, and 358 quayside cranes ; with siding accommodation capable of holding upwards of 55,000 wagons of coal (say, 300 miles of track in sidings only) ; with 68 transit sheds covering about 57 acres of ground ; and with 40 dry docks and pontoons for ship repairs and overhaul. Their combined quayage is about 37 miles.

SWANSEA DOCKS

The Swansea docks are the most extensive of those in South Wales, with $281\frac{1}{2}$ acres of enclosed water space and about 7 miles of quays. From a very early date Swansea was a port, but its facilities consisted only of riverside quays until the middle of last century, when the first of a succession of docks, the North Dock, was completed. This was followed by the South Dock (1859*), which cost £200,000, and was the first ever equipped with hydraulically worked gates ; the Prince of Wales Dock (1891) ; the King's Dock (1909) and the Queen's Dock (1920). In a century the number of ships entering Swansea during a year had increased fourfold, and their total tonnage in a much greater degree. The port's more recent development was due in large measure to the fact that Swansea is the geographical centre of the anthracite coal trade, as well as of an exceedingly busy industrial district. Within a radius of 20 miles

---

* A year or two earlier the South Wales Railway had reached Swansea. It may be said that the subsequent prosperity of the port was due largely to the Great Western Railway.

King's Dock—Swansea.

Oil Tankers in Queen's Dock, Swansea.

of the port are over 500 collieries and works. In 1883, to encourage the use of anthracite abroad, free cargoes were sent to France, Italy, Norway, Sweden and elsewhere. The wisdom of this advertisement is best shown by the fact that, whereas in that year only 509 tons left the port, the annual figures have since gradually risen to 4,000,000 tons. Since 1847 Swansea has specialised in the manufacture of briquettes from coal dust and tar, which are shipped in greater quantities from this port than from any other in the kingdom. Swansea is also one of the world's great metallurgical centres. Within a few miles of the port are produced three-quarters of the tinplates made in this country, for distribution all over the world. A large part of these plates return to Great Britain in the form of containers of meat, fish, fruit and milk. Then, again at or near Swansea are the great zinc refineries capable of handling 90 per cent. of the zinc required in Great Britain ; and other refineries from which come large quantities of nickel and copper sulphate. The most recently established of the Swansea industries is the National Oil Refinery of the Anglo-Persian Oil Company, which deals with crude oil brought in large tankers from the Persian Gulf. This Company took over the great Queen's Dock, 150 acres (about one quarter of a square mile) in extent. It has no quays, but there are several jetties at which tankers discharge the crude oil. The oil is delivered in the first place to one of eight huge transit tanks adjoining the docks, each of which holds 10,000 tons (say 2,500,000 gallons) of oil. From these it is pumped 4 miles through one of six lines of pipes to the tank farm at Llandarcy, for storage in huge holders which have a combined capacity of 75,000,000 gallons. The next ſtage takes it to the refineries, where it is broken up into petrol, lamp oil, lubricating oil, paraffin wax, etc. The liquid elements are ſtored and returned as required through pipes to the dock side, for transference to tankers which carry them by sea to British and Continental ports. Swansea has now become one of the chief oil-distributing centres of the world, though 6,000 miles from the source of production—quite an innovation in the petroleum induſtry—and what but five years ago was bogland and rabbit warrens is now the firſt British equivalent of the great oil-refineries of the United States and Mexico.

The general cargo trade of Swansea has expanded so greatly during the laſt few decades that the port is now one at which many of the leading ſteamship lines call regularly. Swansea has the important advantage over the other South Wales ports of being much nearer the open sea. It is true that during the war its geographical position was a disadvantage as exposing ships to submarine attack; but only from a trading point of view, for the port did very valuable service as the base for patrol vessels, and as a refuge and repair centre for damaged ships.

NEWPORT DOCKS

Newport Docks are the natural outlet for the coals of the Monmouthshire coalfield. They are—except for the small Town Dock—situated in a bend of the river Usk at the point where it enters the Briſtol Channel, and while of less importance than Swansea as regards non-coal exports, do much more handling of coal. The main, or Alexandra, Docks, North and South, form a great L, $123\frac{3}{4}$ acres in extent, the two being joined by a narrow waterway. The

General View of Newport Docks.

South Dock, Newport.

South Dock is a noble sheet of water, connected with the Bristol Channel by a mammoth lock, 1,000 feet long and 100 feet wide, with a maximum depth of water over the outer sill of 45 feet. Intermediate gates can be used to subdivide the lock into an outer portion 400 feet long, and an inner reach of 600 feet. Any ship yet built, with but two or three exceptions, could pass through this greatest of sea locks—opened by H.R.H. Prince Arthur of Connaught on July 14, 1914.

The Docks are splendidly equipped for the loading of coal, much of which comes from famous steam coal collieries only six miles away. As some 6,000,000 tons leave Newport by water annually, much money and much thought have been devoted to facilitating the operations of putting coal aboard ship. There are over 100 miles of sidings, which, when filled with laden trucks awaiting their turn, suggest a sea of coal. Along the inner edge of the great L of the Alexandra docks rise about 20 coal hoists, having lifts of up to 70 feet above quay level. Trucks approach a hoist by lines at right angles to the quay, and each is lifted in turn, discharged through end doors into a shoot with an anti-breakage box at the lower end to catch the coal, and run off on to an elevated track, down which it travels by gravity to the sidings. Every wagon is weighed both when approaching and leaving a hoist, so that its load is given by simple subtraction. The "Newport Way" of coal-loading is indicated by the transference of 10,650 tons to the s.s. *Algoa* in 36 hours. Newport is less than 100 miles from Birmingham, and its proximity to the Midlands should be a big factor in its future development.

BRUNEL AND AFTER

Barry Docks, which came into the Great Western group along with the Barry Railway, have an area of but 114 acres, yet they hold the record for shipping coal, some ten million tons of which are exported from the port in a year. The largest tonnage shipped during a twelve-month is 11,049,711; the record day shipment 55,840 tons; and the record weekly shipment 254,726. These figures speak for themselves as to the importance of Barry, which lies 20 miles west of Cardiff. The docks are comparatively new ones, as the Act for their construction was obtained only in 1884, and the growth of trade done in them has been phenomenal. To cope with the coal traffic, over 100 miles of sidings have been provided; also 41 coal hoists of the most modern type and of high capacity. Six hundred tons of coal can be put aboard in an hour—an ordinary truck load every minute. The hoists, as well as all other machinery in the docks, are worked by hydraulic power generated by 12 steam engines of 250 h.p. each—6,000 h.p. in all. Water at a pressure of 750 lb. per square inch is pumped into the cylinders of 15 hydraulic accumulators, connected by a system of piping with the various points at which power is needed. The accumulators act as reservoirs of energy, to do away with the need for constant pumping and to assure uniform pressure. The water pumped into a cylinder raises the heavily-weighted ram until it attains a certain height, when the engine feeding the accumulator is automatically slowed down. Similarly, if it sinks below a certain level, the engine, which is more than able to deal with the greatest possible demands on it, begins pumping again. So the

No. 1 Dock—Barry.

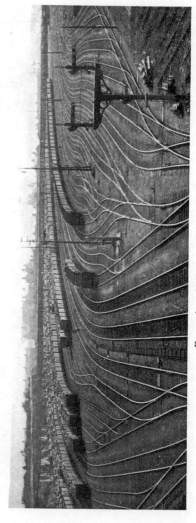

Reception Sidings at Barry Docks.

cylinder can neither be overfilled nor emptied, and is always at the service of any machine connected with it. Hydraulic power has the advantages of silence and great steadiness in action, water being practically incompressible.

Considerations of space preclude further reference to the Great Western Railway docks in Wales, but sufficient has been said to give some idea of their importance as sea outlets and inlets to the territory served by the railway system in which we are interested.

INTRODUCTION OF HIGH CAPACITY WAGONS.

In co-operation with traders, to secure more economical and efficient transport of coal, the Great Western Railway

New Standard 20-ton Mineral Wagon.

successfully initiated in August, 1924, the adoption of a

20-ton wagon as the new standard for the conveyance of shipment coal in South Wales. The new wagon, considerable numbers of which are now in use, is destined to take the place of the 10- and 12-ton wagon; and apart from export coal there is every indication that the bigger wagon will also be utilised for inland coal, roadstone, and other minerals. The benefits accruing to the trader are substantial (apart from reduced construction and maintenance costs, increased capacity of sidings, etc.), the G.W.R. allow a rebate of 5 per cent. off the conveyance rate and a further reduction of 1¼d. per ton in tipping and weighing charges on coal conveyed in fully loaded 20-ton wagons over their line.

THE GREAT WESTERN AND THE "CITY"

The Metropolitan Railway, which in 1854 was incorporated to construct a sub-surface line from Bishop's Road to Farringdon Street, had a useful ally in the Great Western Railway. It may be news to many users of the " Metro " that, when the railway was opened on January 10, 1863, it was a mixed-gauge line, and was operated as broad-gauge by the G.W.R. for six months. Friction then developed between the companies, and the Metropolitan was subsequently worked as a narrow-gauge line, the outer rails being removed in 1869. The association was not, however, completely severed, as the Hammersmith and City Railway from Hammersmith to Westbourne Park, constructed by an independent company and opened in 1864, has been jointly owned by the two companies ever since 1868, and the Great Western still runs " through " trains from its main line over the Metropolitan from

Bishop's Road to Liverpool Street, the change-over from electric to steam traction, or *vice versa*, being made at the former station. It need hardly be said that this through service is of very great convenience to thousands of people who live in the suburban districts served by the G.W.R., but have their business in the " City."

THE EALING AND SHEPHERD'S BUSH RAILWAY

This second link between the Great Western Railway and the City of London was opened on August 3, 1920. Constructed and owned by the G.W.R., it may be regarded as a westward extension of the Central London Railway, since it provides a through service of electric trains from Ealing to Liverpool Street.

Though only a little over four miles long, the railway involved some considerable engineering work, since for nearly the whole of its length the rails are either in a deep cutting or on the top of an embankment. Over 600,000 cubic yards of earth had to be excavated to make the cuttings, and of this quantity about one third was utilised for the embankments, which attain a maximum height at East Acton Station. In order to reach Ealing, the northern side of the cutting east of the Broadway station had to be cut away, and held up by a heavy retaining wall : and nineteen bridges were needed, fifteen of which cross over the line. These were designed to allow of quadrupling the track should it become necessary to do so.

Soon after leaving Ealing the railway bears away northeastwards for a mile till it reaches the steam track from Old Oak Common to High Wycombe, along the south side of which it runs eastwards for a mile or so. Points and crossings make connection between the two to allow steam trains to be diverted on to the electric track at Willesden

A " Flying Junction."

Lane. Beyond North Acton Station the line dives under the G.W.R. main line, and runs on an embankment past Wormwood Scrubs to East Acton, where the facilities given by it have brought into existence a new suburb. Beyond this point is seen an interesting engineering feature—a " flying junction "—which was needed in order to make the " up " and " down " tracks fit in with those of the Central London at Wood Lane. After leaving East Acton the " up " track falls gradually, while the down remains an embankment until the difference in height makes it possible for the " down " to cross the " up " by a skew bridge, beyond which the down falls gradually to the level of the other, but on the " wrong " side of it.

The gradient down to the Wood Lane Station is very steep—1 in 54—and in order to prevent it being even more severe it was necessary to raise the level of Wood Lane, which crosses the railway half a mile west of the Central London terminal station. As this is a very busy thoroughfare a temporary diversion had to be made while a new bridge and approaches were under construction.

A little westwards of the " flying junction " referred to above, the " up " track throws off a branch northwards, along which steam trains may pass to a junction with the West London Railway at Viaduct Junction. This arrangement gives direct connection between the West London Railway and the " short cut " to High Wycombe and Birmingham, by means of the electric track, which, as has

Ealing and Shepherd's Bush Railway, Ealing.
Broadway Station.

already been pointed out, has a junction with the short-cut at Willesden Lane.

BRUNEL AND AFTER

The Ealing and Shepherd's Bush Railway was planned as long ago as 1905, and had been practically finished, apart from electrification and the building of stations, in 1914. The outbreak of war brought operations to a standstill, though on April 16, 1917, part of the line was opened for goods traffic. On the conclusion of peace electrification was pushed forward and stations were built at Ealing and East Acton, prior to the opening in 1920. Since then further stations have been provided at West Acton and North Acton (opened November 5, 1923), giving residents in their neighbourhood the advantages of a train every ten minutes to or from the very heart of the City.

THE INCREASE IN COMFORT, SPEED AND SAFETY OF TRAVEL ON THE GREAT WESTERN RAILWAY

WHEN a railway traveller of to-day sets out on a long journey he takes it for granted that he will reach his destination without mishap, and, except at certain " rush " seasons, with reasonable punctuality.   He can assume also that, so far as the rolling stock is concerned, his surroundings will be comfortable ; though, of course, he cannot ensure immunity from the idiosyncrasies of his fellow passengers—the " fresh-air " fanatic, for example, who usually, by the bye, occupies a corner seat and has his (or her) back to the engine !

It will, perhaps, induce philosophy in those readers who are apt to pick holes in the organisation of the traffic department, to review the gradual development of coaching stock by the Great Western Railway.

When the early railways were planned, the Boards of Directors undoubtedly had their eyes chiefly on the people who used the stage coach and post chaise.   It was assumed that, if a superior class of carriage were provided for the chaise folk and the " insides," with a less luxurious class for those who were contented to travel outside the coaches, anyone desiring cheaper quarters should be content with conditions such as the driver and fireman had for long to endure. In other words, the third-class passenger was regarded as very small beer indeed and hardly worth troubling about. Should he persist in travelling, there was the truck for him, without covering of any kind and, perhaps, seatless, though possibly a few cross planks might be provided. And, naturally, he must not expect to travel at first or second-class speeds, but at the extremely moderate gait of a goods train, when one was available. Many years had to elapse before the supreme importance to passenger traffic returns of the third-class was realised.

THIRD CLASS EIGHTY YEARS AGO

Imagine that, for your sins, you had been obliged to travel third class from London to Exeter in the year of grace 1845, Bradshaw's time-table for which lies open before the writer. On the right hand side of the single page devoted to G.W.R. " down " trains, are two columns, separated by a heavy vertical rule from the other columns, and headed " 3rd class." If you selected the 9.30 a.m.—the 6.30 a.m. ran only as far as Bristol—you reached Didcot at 12.45 p.m., Swindon at 2.15 p.m., and Bristol at 5.20 p.m. There you cooled your heels till 7.0 p.m., when the second stage of the journey began, to end at 12.30 a.m. the following morning. The average speed of about 13 miles an hour conforms, be it noted, with Mr. Gladstone's Parliamentary train Act of 1844, under which third-class passengers had to be guaranteed a minimum average speed of 12 miles an hour, stoppages included. The same Act also ensured the passenger a covered carriage—of a box-like, unwindowed kind—and a seat. What his experiences would have been prior to that measure coming into force is so painful a consideration that we prefer to revert to the more pleasant subject of the " upper classes."

Here is a first hand account of some of the rolling-stock with which the Great Western was opened :—" We, the other day, paid a visit to Paddington, to see some of the Company's carriages, of whose splendour we had heard so much that we thought the Directors had sunk all regard for the proprietors in reckless extravagance. We, however, found nothing to justify our anticipations. The carriages are made very comfortable, but nothing more. Those we saw of the first class have three double bodies, holding each very comfortably four persons. One had four double bodies. The bodies of the former measured 18 feet long, 6 feet high, and $8\frac{1}{4}$ feet wide ; the frame below was $1\frac{1}{2}$ feet deeper. They run on four wheels, 4 feet high, except the four double-bodied one, which runs on six. The dimensions of the second-class carriages are the same, and the difference is, that they consist of three single bodies, comfortable, but without cushions or padded backs and sides. We think these carriages preferable to the second class on the Grand Junction, and that the springs in each class are better adapted to the work they will have to do than any we have yet seen."[*]

To judge by Frith's celebrated picture of Paddington Station—which, when first exhibited, created such a *furore* that it had to be roped off—there was not much alteration till the late 'fifties in the design of passenger coaches. The picture shows the baggage being placed on the

[*] *Herepath's Railway Magazine, March,* 1838.

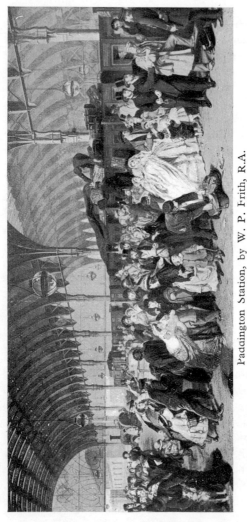

Paddington Station, by W. P. Frith, R.A.

The original picture, which hangs in the Art Gallery of the Royal Holloway College, Egham, was painted by W. P. Frith, R.A., in 1862, he having been commissioned to do so by L. V. Flatow, picture dealer of the Haymarket. The canvas measures 8 feet 5 inches by 3 feet 10 inches. The artist received £4,500 for his work, plus £750 for waiving his right to send it for exhibition to the Royal Academy, to admit of it being separately exhibited at Flatow's Gallery, where 21,150 people paid for admission to view it in seven weeks. It was exhibited in 1878 at the International Exhibition in Paris, and also in 1924 in the Palace of Arts at the British Empire Exhibition, Wembley.

carriage roofs—where it was liable to be damaged by stray cinders—as the idea of separate baggage vans had not yet penetrated to official quarters.

Up till 1845, at anyrate, you might, if you liked, travel in your own road carriage, run on a flat truck. "Bradshaw" of that year gives the schedule of charges. Thus, for conveyance of a 4-wheeled carriage from Paddington to Bristol a sum of 58/- was levied, and 53/- for a single horse, or 73/- for a pair. Presumably the owner paid first-class fare whether he travelled in his own conveyance or aboard the train. In the former manner, you may remember, journeyed the immortal Mr. Jorrocks, to Handley Cross in the Vale of Sheepwash.

THE FIRST ROYAL SALOON

A special effort was, of course, made in anticipation of Queen Victoria taking to the railway, as she did for the

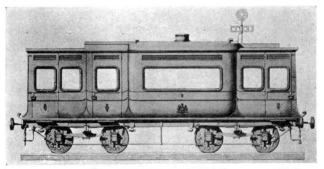

Queen Victoria's Carriage, 1850.

first time in 1842. The original Royal carriage built in

1840, was but 21 feet long, and divided into three compartments, the central one nearly 12 feet long. It had large windows and was carried on four pairs of wooden-tyred wheels—a somewhat dangerous practice, one would imagine !

Until 1867 private contractors supplied the necessary rolling stock. From this time onwards improvements followed one another fairly rapidly. By 1871 the length of coaches had been increased to 31 feet ; and in 1874 appeared a 46-foot 8-wheeled coach. About this period the lighting of trains by flickering oil lamps gave way to the use of gas, compressed in cylinders, and burners of a more or less crude type. The much needed provision of lavatories on long distance trains began in 1882, when a few first-class vehicles were so equipped. The third-class passenger, whose importance could no longer be denied, had also to be catered for, and in 1892 we find third-class carriages on all trains, fast or slow. The same year is notable in Great Western annals for the putting into service of the first corridor train for all classes—the first three-class train of the kind in the country. The coaches were from 50 to 56 feet long, all contained lavatories, and generally were a great advance on any yet put on to Great Western rails.

Those of us who can remember when to travel in frosty weather meant windows coated with ice, and how grateful one was even for the clumsy footwarmer, can best appreciate what the introduction of steam heating of coaches in 1893 meant to passengers. Thick ulsters and heavy rugs no longer were essential to comfort. The next improvement concerned itself with the inner, rather than the outer man ; for with 1896 appeared the dining car—first-class

Early Third Class Carriage.

Modern Third Class Carriage.

only as a beginning. The closing year of the century saw an ordinary train equipped with electric light, which previously had been confined to a Royal train. In 1900 the third-class travellers got their dining cars, and in 1905 incandescent gas illumination came in. The abolition of second-class fares altogether in 1910 marks the final triumph for the third-class passenger. What would a traveller by the 15-hour Exeter " slow " of 1845 think if he found himself in one of the new main line express trains ? He would hardly be able to believe that there had ever been a time when—as is related of a railway *not* the Great Western—sweeps were hired, and sheep or pigs compelled to enter third-class carriages to drive out all who were mean enough to use such carriages though, in the opinion of the Company, possessing the means for higher fares. The miserable pens or hutches, or whatever one likes to call them, have given place to palatial cars 70 feet long and 9 feet wide, draught-proof, but efficiently ventilated by scientifically designed air-extractors. In the white enamelled ceiling of each compartment are three electric lamps, and under the seats heaters that can be controlled independently by the passengers. The upholstery leaves nothing to be desired, and the large windows give as good a view of the country as can reasonably be demanded. Passing down the corridor, our visitor would be astonished to find a complete kitchen and pantry, and beyond these the third-class dining saloon, with accommodation for 32 diners. Imagine his wonder at the tip-up leather-covered seats, the tables spread with snowy linen, the carpeted floor, the polished mahogany panels, and other things, such as the electric fans and bell-pushes, which would require some explanation. What could Royalty itself have asked in the early period of railway travel that the user of such a train as this does not enjoy to-day?

Interior of Restaurant Car.

THE GROWTH OF SPEED

Since the primary object of a railway is to transport people and commodities from one place to another at the highest speed consistent with safe and profitable working, the development of speed on the Great Western would appear to merit at least brief notice in a "history book."

A comparison of early with present-day speeds is apt to be very misleading if certain factors are not taken into account. The first of them is the weight of the trains moved. The Report issued by the Railway Commissioners in 1846 (see p. 64) contained some interesting figures as to the weight of trains then running on the G.W.R. system. " The average weight," says the Report, " of a passenger train on the Great Western Railway (independent of the engine and tender, which weighs 33 tons) appears to be 67 tons ; and the average number of passengers per train for the half-year ending June 30, 1845, is only 47.2, whilst the weight, including their luggage, may be estimated at about 5 tons." This refers to the London-Bristol traffic. On the Oxford branch a train averaged 48 tons, on the Cheltenham branch, 46 tons ; between Swindon and Bristol, 60 tons ; and on the Bristol and Exeter railway, 53 tons.

In comparison with the 300-400 tons of the crack expresses of to-day these figures seem very small. In fact it was the lightness of the trains which enabled Daniel Gooch to use the " 8-foot singles," which made so good a showing in the 'forties, when, under the stimulus of a threatened invasion of the western counties by the London and South Western Railway, the morning Exeter express was scheduled to do the 77 miles from Paddington to Swindon in 85 minutes—an average speed of 56.7 miles an hour.

Other factors favouring high speed were the comparative fewness of trains, and the rapidity with which velocity could be regained after a stop : though this last advantage was, it is only fair to say, more or less cancelled out by the slowness of stopping when a few hand-applied brakes had to be relied upon, and by the less perfect signalling system.

Beyond a doubt the old broad-gauge engines designed by Gooch as a challenge to the powerful contemporary narrow-gauge locomotives were very fine examples of mechanical engineering, even without making allowance for the comparatively imperfect—as judged by standards of to-day—machine-tools used in their construction. The first of the series, and one of the first to be built in the (then) recently opened works at Swindon, was very suitably named the " Great Western." This engine was credited with many very fast long runs averaging well over 50, and reaching at times the neighbourhood of 80 miles an hour. Another famous locomotive was the " Lord of the Isles," which travelled nearly 800,000 miles before her boiler was renewed, and did regular service for thirty years.

" Lord of the Isles."

During the " fifties " the best express speeds retrograded somewhat, though the opening of the London-Oxford-Birmingham route, in 1852, might have been expected to make the G.W.R. show what it could do in the way of cutting down the rival London and North Western times. In 1861, however, the London and South Western Railway reached Exeter, and in this case the challenge was taken up, the " Flying Dutchman " now making its appearance. This train left Paddington at 11.45, and was timed to run to Didcot at an average speed of 56 miles an hour—not quite so good as the record of 1848 as regards time, but probably more meritorious when the greater weight of the trains is taken into consideration. Originally this train ran only to Exeter, but in 1865 its journey was extended to Plymouth, with a slow connection on the Cornwall and West Cornwall railways. Two years later it was taken off for a year, and when put on again in 1869 it took $4\frac{3}{4}$ instead of the old $4\frac{1}{2}$ hours to reach Exeter, until the original timing was restored in 1871.

Though a second train was, in 1880, added to the schedule at 3.0 p.m., known as the " Zulu," to duplicate the morning " Dutchman," no long distance runs at over 53 miles an hour were registered till 1902, by which time the Great Western had fallen behind some of the other lines. In the year just mentioned, three " down " and one " up " trains between London and Birmingham did the distance of $129\frac{1}{4}$ miles in 140 minutes, non-stop, which works out at $55\frac{1}{2}$ miles per hour. But soon afterwards, in 1903, the London-Bristol $118\frac{1}{4}$ mile run was turned off daily by four trains in 120 minutes " dead," which equals a fraction over 59 miles an hour, the highest " scheduled " speed yet attained on the Great Western—and, be it noted, with trains that ten years earlier would have been considered heavy.

THE CORNISH RIVIERA EXPRESS

The year 1904 saw the inauguration of what was then, and, twenty-one years later, still is, the longest non-stop run in the world. A train left Paddington daily at 10.10 a.m., and did not come to a standstill—unless, of course, pulled up by signals—till it reached Plymouth, 245½ miles away, 265 minutes later. An average speed of 55½ miles an hour for such a distance was remarkable, considering the stiffness of the gradients to be climbed between Taunton and Exeter, and between Newton Abbot and Plymouth. The " Cornish Riviera Express," as it is now called—also the " 10.30 Limited," since the starting time has been put back 20 minutes—now does the journey in 247 minutes, not travelling faster, but following the shorter route *via* Westbury and Castle Cary (see p. 102). It takes eight minutes less to reach Plymouth than the " 3.0 p.m." took to reach Exeter in 1880. Nor does its journey terminate at Plymouth, for, true to its name of " *Cornish* Riviera Express," it carries on to the very end of the line at Penzance, which it reaches in 6½ hours from London. Its " opposite number " leaves Penzance at 10 a.m. and reaches Paddington in 6¾ hours. The " up " journey is not non-stop between Plymouth and London, as the train calls at Exeter. What this 305-mile journey in 6½ hours means can be appreciated only by making it, as the bare figures do not suggest how wonderful it is, especially west of Exeter. The train as it leaves Paddington is a very heavy one. On April 2, 1925, for example, there were 11 coaches, weighing 35-38 tons apiece ; a 40-ton restaurant car and an iron baggage car :—say 450 tons behind the engine. If the writer's watch is to be relied upon the times registered on that particular date were :—

Westbury	(95 miles)	-	98	minutes from start
Frome	(101 miles)	-	106	,, ,,
Taunton	(143 miles)	-	147½	,, ,,
Plymouth	(226 miles)	-	247	,, ,,

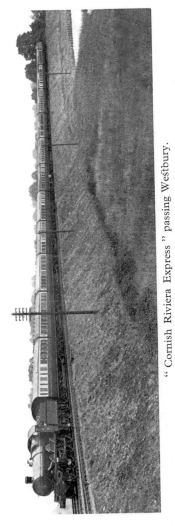

"Cornish Riviera Express" passing Westbury.

True, some coaches had been dropped before Taunton was passed and the load thus considerably reduced when the train reached the formidable incline to Whiteball Tunnel; and at Exeter two more were slipped, but the work remained heavy enough to tax the locomotive hard both through Whiteball and up to Dainton, beyond Totnes, and again on the stiff grade leading up to Brent. Allowance must also be made for service slacks at various points.

As for the 80 miles beyond Plymouth, covered in 136 minutes (35.3 miles an hour), the performance here is no less meritorious, as the country crossed—the uplands of Cornwall—is a regular switchback, and the line a succession of curves and stiff gradients. Moreover, three stops have to be made before Penzance is reached. The Great Western Railway therefore has good reason to be proud of the " 10.30 Limited."

Times from London to South Wales have recently been reduced. Newport ($133\frac{1}{2}$ miles) is now reached in 140 minutes, non-stop, the average speed being 57.2 miles an hour; while Fishguard, $268\frac{1}{2}$ miles from Paddington, is only 355 minutes away (6 intermediate stops).

The Great Western Railway has, in the 2.30 p.m. " up " from Cheltenham, the train which makes the fastest non-stop run in the British Isles. It is booked to leave Swindon at 3.45 p.m., and to reach Paddington ($77\frac{1}{4}$ miles) at 5.0 p.m., which means an average speed of 61.8 miles an hour. On its first run it actually averaged $64\frac{1}{4}$ miles an hour, the load being nine coaches, weighing 250 tons, and the maximum speed 83 miles an hour.

It should be noted that the times given are the *booked* times and, fast as they are, they by no means represent the maximum speeds attained. Every now and then re-markable runs are made by " specials "—mails, boat trains, etc.—usually lighter than the regular trains.

Thus, on July 14, 1903, the " City of Bath " took a Royal Special (130 tons) from Paddington to Plymouth, *via* Bristol, at an average speed of 63.14 m.p.h. This beat all previous records. About two years later an Ocean special made the trip in the opposite direction in 3 hours 46 minutes 48 seconds, averaging 65.49 m.p.h. On the decline east of Whiteball Tunnel the speed rose to 102.3 m.p.h., the fastest " clocked " speed registered by a steam train.

Even these speeds do not represent the highest possible that could be attained " regardless of cost." There is an old story of an engine driver who, in the early days, offered to take a train from London to Bristol in an hour if per-mission were given by the Directors. This sporting offer was turned down, for obvious reasons. It would no doubt be feasible to run average speeds up to 70 or even 75 m.p.h., but such speeds would not " pay," and in these days, more than ever before, quickness of transport has to be balanced carefully against economy in running.

SIGNALS

The very early employment of the electric telegraph by the Great Western Railway has already been alluded to. Its usefulness for regulating traffic and preventing acci-dents developed simultaneously with improvements in signalling apparatus and safety devices and the general system of line control of which it forms part.

The comparative immunity from serious accidents that railways enjoyed in the pioneer days—the Great Western's casualty list for the first three years of working was but one broken leg and a few bruises among over three million passengers—was due mainly to the fewness of the trains running. In 1845 only 19 trains left Paddington, at intervals of about an hour, during a day, whereas the number now is about 170. When, on special occasions, an unusually large number of people had to be transported, it seems to have been the practice to make up a very long train, hauled by several engines, rather than multiply the number of trains ; probably because the fewer there were on the line the safer things would be.

Under these simple conditions very primitive methods of signalling served well enough. The earliest signalman was a railway policeman* in tight-buttoned tail coat and, of course, the inevitable official top hat of the period. In place of a baton he carried a red, a green, and a white flag ; or, at night, a lamp with suitably coloured lenses.

With these and his arms he gave the engine driver what information he could. He was also responsible for operating such fixed signals as were provided. The earliest consisted of a kind of gallows from which hung a ball. When the ball was raised as high as possible, it indicated " Safety " ; when lowered, " Danger." At night a lantern replaced the ball. A somewhat more elaborate contrivance used on the Great Western was the " kite "—a semi-circular iron frame fixed on the top of a post. By pulling a string, the signalman could fill the space inside the frame more or less completely with a canvas curtain. Thus, a quadrant of canvas meant " Caution " ; a semi-circle, " Danger " ; and no canvas at all, " All Clear."

* A signalman is still known colloquially as a " bobby."

At some period between 1840 and 1845 the Great Western adopted the disc-and-crossbar signal—a revolving vertical pole with a large disc at the top for " Safety," and below,

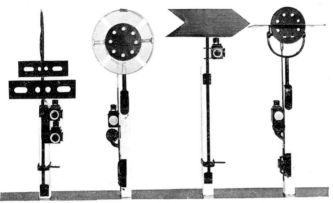

Disc and Crossbar Signals.

and at right angles to, the disc, a long cross board, for " Danger." This kind of signal was reported on very favourably by the Government Inspector of Railways. In 1847 signals were further differentiated by attaching short horns above the crossbars relating to the " up " line, and below those controlling the " down " line.

SEMAPHORE SIGNALS

In 1842 the first *semaphore* signal, such as is used to-day, was erected at New Cross, on the London and Croydon Railway ; for the resident engineer of that line had conceived the idea of applying to railway purposes a device which had long been employed for military and naval signalling. The Great Western Railway apparently did not take up the semaphore until the 'sixties. At first three positions were used—the arm horizontal, for " Danger " ; the arm lowered to an angle of 45 degrees, for "Caution " ; the arm lowered vertically, for " All Clear." The " Caution " position was abandoned by the Great Western in 1871, and " All Clear " indicated, as now, by lowering to an angle of 60 degrees.

For night work a lamp was provided, with red, green, and white lenses. This was at first operated independently of the arm. But in due course appeared the " spectacle frame," attached to the pivot end of the semaphore arm to ensure arm and lamp giving the same signal. Semaphores were restricted for some time to " stop " (Home and Starting) signals, the disc being retained for Distant or cautionary signals ; and even when they displaced discs some years elapsed before Distant signals were differentiated from Stop by the characteristic notched or fishtail end now used.

LEVER FRAMES

Somewhere about the year 1850 a beginning was made with the concentration in one place of all the levers for working the signals at a station, to relieve the signalman of a great deal of walking and to give him fuller and quicker control. It was a simple enough matter to connect the signals with their respective levers by means of wires. A similar concentration of levers operating points came into use about the same time—no exact dates are available : and the next step was the grouping of both signal and points levers in one frame, and providing them with *interlocking gear*. This device has been of immense value for preventing accidents by rendering impossible the giving of conflicting signals and the operation of point and signal levers in the wrong order. In the period 1860-1870 the Great Western Railway, which had established special signal works at Reading in 1859, began to equip its whole system

Interior of Signal Box.

with interlocked lever frames. The first frame of this kind was placed at Paddington in 1860 ; and the first completely interlocked frame at Taplow in 1872. The gradual increase in the number of levers in individual signal boxes, and consequently in the space required, led to the introduction of " power " signalling equipments, with miniature levers which merely turn on the power that does the hard work of moving points and signals. Didcot North box (opened 1905) and three other large boxes are now operated on the " all electric " system, which, besides economising space, increases safety by giving the signalman a positive indication in the box when the movement of a lever has had its proper effect.

BRUNEL AND AFTER

AUDIBLE SIGNALLING

Readers have probably noticed at various places between Paddington and Reading, bars 40 or so feet long fixed between, and parallel to, the rails of a track, and may have wondered what their purpose is. They are "ramps" employed to inform an engine driver whether the Distant signal near by is at "Danger" or "All Clear." A ramp is slightly curved, being $1\frac{1}{2}$ inch higher at the middle than at the ends.

the ends. When an engine runs over it, a shoe on the engine is raised, operating electrical apparatus in the cab. Should the signal be at "All Clear," an electric bell is set ringing and continues to ring until switched off by the driver. Should, however, the signal be at "Danger," the whistle blows until silenced. In either case the driver gets audible information which cannot pass unnoticed. The ramp is insulated and connected with a battery in the

Engine Passing over Ramp.

signal box. The lowering of the distant signal renders the ramp "alive"; otherwise it remains "dead"; and its condition determines whether the whistle or the bell shall sound. This "Audible Signalling," or "Driver's Cab Signal" system was installed first on the Henley branch, in

1906 ; on the Fairford branch the same year ; on the Paddington-Reading section in 1908 ; and on the Lambourn Valley branch in 1909. Its special advantages are the persistence and definiteness of the signals, by night and by day, and the giving of information in weather which might render the semaphore signals quite invisible. The value of audible signals in fog is self-evident.

View in Engine Cab shewing Audible Signal Apparatus.

THE BLOCK SYSTEM

In the days when traffic was thin, a time interval between trains was regarded as a sufficient safeguard. But with the multiplication of trains, and especially of goods trains, some more positive method of combating the effects of drivers not being able to see round corners or through darkness became imperative. One of the inventors of the electric telegraph, Mr. W. F. Cooke, suggested that a railway should be divided up into sections or lengths, each protected by signals ; and that only one train should be allowed to be in one section at any time. Under these conditions the likelihood of collisions would be greatly diminished. The electric telegraph provided an ideal means of enabling the signalmen responsible for the various sections to keep in touch with one another and set their signals correctly.

Officials were at first opposed to the " block " system—as it came to be called—since it seemed likely to delay the working of trains—though, in fact, it had exactly the opposite effect. But in 1850 a trial was made with the " absolute block " system on the section including the Box Tunnel, where exceptional precautions were needed. During the next few years some other sections were equipped. The mode of working used was, however, somewhat crude and left a good deal to the " human element." In 1855, Mr. C. E. Spagnoletti was appointed Telegraph Superintendent of the Great Western Railway, and soon afterwards he evolved his three-position disc block instrument. This was first put into use at two places, in 1863, and has since (with improvements) become standard throughout the Great Western system. Even as early as 1877 the block system was operating 1,374 miles of track.

Block instruments are used in pairs, a pair for each track, in every box. One of a pair has two keys, the other has none. In the face of each is a small window, behind which moves a two-part " flag," bearing on one half the words,

" Train On Line," in white letters on a red ground, and on the other, " Line Clear," in black letters on a white ground. Each key on the keyed instrument controls one

indication. When neither key is held down (by means of a sliding wire) the flag is in mid or normal position, with parts of both indications showing. The main points of the block system are, first, that the keyed instrument of one signal box is connected with the keyless instrument in the preceding box, and the two are electrically coupled so as to work together and give similar indications; and, second, that a signalman must not use his keyed instrument to give permission to the box in the rear (that is, on the side from which a train is approaching),nor ask permission by

Combined Key Disc and Keyless Disc Instrument.

bell signal from the box ahead, unless the keyless instrument, over which he has no control, warrants him in doing so. The Spagnoletti system of working does not eliminate entirely the possibility of making mistakes, but it goes a long way towards doing so.

SINGLE LINE WORKING

For working *single* lines special provisions are needed, to prevent two trains entering a section at opposite ends at the same time. In the early days trains on single lines ran to a schedule which assigned certain places for passing. But it will easily be understood that the schedules were frequently upset by trains getting behind time. Various methods of overcoming this trouble were tried, and in 1867 the Great Western Railway adopted the Train Staff and Ticket system. A single staff, of a distinguishing shape and colour, is assigned to each section, and a driver on entering a section must be given the staff as his authority to proceed. When leaving the section he surrenders the staff, and receives that for the next section. Since the drivers of two trains cannot possibly possess the same staff at the same time, adherence to the system definitely prevents two trains being in the same section at once.

To allow for two or more trains following one another through a section, each staff may be supplemented by "tickets," which can be withdrawn from the boxes in which they are kept only with the aid of the staff. As long as there are any tickets left, trains can follow one another, provided the staff itself has not been taken. A driver must not accept a ticket unless he actually *sees* the staff, and so is certain that the staff has not gone ahead. Even the tickets do not prevent a staff occasionally being at the wrong end of a section when wanted and having to be brought back by hand. In 1891, therefore, the Great Western Railway adopted for their busier single lines the Electric Staff System. At the end of a section are two electrically inter-controlled staffholders, able to accommodate a large number of staffs, any one of which would be accepted by a driver. A staff can be withdrawn from either holder only when *all* the staffs are in the holders. Assuming 20 staffs to be allotted to a section, if 11 are at one end and 9 at the other, or 6 at one end and 14 at the other, a staff can be removed. When it is out, there will be an " even " number of staffs at one end and an " odd " number at the other, and the releasing mechanism will refuse to work until the restoration of the staff makes both numbers " even " or " odd," as the case may be.

Electric Train Staff Instrument.

BRAKES

For many years after they first began running, passenger as well as goods trains carried no brakes other than the hand brakes on the engine and in the guard's van that could be applied while the train was in motion. The procedure of checking a passenger train was, there-fore, during this period practically the same as that of slowing an ordinary coal train to-day. But, as the trains were comparatively short and light, and few and far between, the risks run were not so serious as they would be to-day.

As passenger trains became heavier, and the frequency of trains greater, various devices were tried for applying brakes simultaneously to every vehicle.

During the 'seventies two types of " automatic continu-ous " brakes appeared—the compressed-air Westinghouse

187

and the Vacuum. Both made it possible to apply braking power evenly to all the wheels of a train—hence the term " continuous " ; and both came into action automatically if any vehicle should break away, the brakes being applied both to the detached and to the undetached portions. The driver thus got indisputable proof of " something having happened."

The Great Western, like most other British railways, selected the Vacuum brake, which was first fitted to its passenger rolling stock in 1875 or thereabouts. Since then it has been improved to its present state of perfection, and is found on all coaching stock and on many goods trucks and vans of the G.W.R. It need hardly be said that the continuous brake increases the safety of fast travel immensely, as it can arrest a train moving at high speed in its own length. It would probably not be going beyond the truth to say that a train could be taken into Paddington Station at fifty miles an hour at the platform ends and be brought to a standstill before the engine reached the hydraulic stop-buffers. But it would be an uncomfortable experiment for the passengers !

Stated very briefly, the principle of the Vacuum Brake is this. Every vehicle carries a vertical cylinder, the piston whereof is connected with the brake gear of the vehicle : and all the cylinders of the train are in communication with a pipe running the whole length of the train.

A steam air-ejector on the locomotive exhausts air from the pipe and from the cylinders, both above and below the pistons, which fall by their own weight, leaving the brakes free. Should the driver or the guard open a valve, or the train break apart, air rushes into the pipe and into the lower part only of every cylinder. A valve prevents it *entering*, though permitting it to be exhausted from, the space above the piston. Consequently atmospheric pressure forces the piston up, applying the brakes, which can be released only by exhausting the air again or by admitting air to the space above the piston by means of a lever fitted for the purpose.

We have, in more senses than one, journeyed a long way since the days of the " travelling porter " who sat at the back of the tender of a G.W.R. locomotive, facing the train. His job was (among other things) to keep an eye on the train, and to inform the driver should anything untoward happen—such as the dismemberment of the train. His was a thankless duty, though he was better off than the unfortunate fore and after guards of trains on other railways, who sat facing the engine on top of their vans at the head and tail of the train. Even in the open they must have been kept busy dodging cinders, and in the tunnels—but perhaps when they saw one ahead they were allowed to scramble down from their perches !

SOME FACTS AND FIGURES

I N 1842 the mileage of the Great Western Railway totalled about 120 miles of double track, and the number of locomotives was 59.

During the second half of the previous year 882,119 passengers were carried, their fares totalling £275,025; while the revenue from the carriage of merchandise and parcels was £46,774 for the first and £15,208 for the second.

Passenger returns for the following years were :—

1843	-	-	-	1,629,250
1844	-	-	-	1,791,272
1845	-	-	-	2,441,255

By 1859 the rolling stock had increased to comparatively imposing figures : for, taking that for both broad and narrow gauge together, we find on the list :—

403 Locomotives ;	1,204 Open Wagons ;
216 First-class Carriages ;	1,946 Closed ditto ;
100 Composite ditto ;	4,114 Coal ditto ;
273 Second-class ditto ;	
157 Third-class ditto.	

The smallness of the number of third-class carriages is an interesting indication of the relatively minor importance of this class.

SOME FACTS AND FIGURES

To realise the present-day magnitude and activities of the Great Western Railway, one cannot do better than refer to the latest Report issued—that for the year ending December 31, 1924. With the help of an apparently dry mass of figures it is possible to arrive at a good deal of interesting and illuminating information.

Beginning with *mileage*, the actual geographical length of lines totals 3,648 miles; but, as there are 1,880 miles of second, 278 miles of third, 175 miles of fourth, and 110 miles of fifth track, the total mileage, expressed in terms of single track, comes to 8,387, sidings included: or, with leased and jointly-owned lines, 8,742. This mileage would suffice for a continuous single line from London to Vladivostok and thence to Calcutta. The rails represent about $1\frac{1}{4}$ million tons of steel, the chairs 800,000 tons of cast iron, and the sleepers 50,000,000 cubic feet of timber.

The *passenger vehicles*, giving seating accommodation for 39,510 first-class and 315,128 third-class passengers, number 6,775; and with them may be associated 3,418 other coaching vehicles. *Goods vehicles* total 87,624, and include 57,325 open wagons, 17,299 covered wagons, 3,106 cattle trucks, and 2,401 brake vans. If coupled in a continuous string they would reach from London to Edinburgh.

To haul this gigantic goods train the Great Western Railway could muster 3,996 locomotives, with 1,574 tenders, which would occupy another 35 miles of track.

For handling goods on the roads 4,556 vehicles, requiring the services of 2,706 horses, are employed; while 123 passenger motor vehicles ply on road routes in connection with the railway. At the terminal ports and harbours we find 16 steamers, having a total registered tonnage of 6,471 and a combined horse-power of 56,900—which means that they have a very high turn of speed. In passing, it may be mentioned that there are 17 docks and harbours with 37 miles of quay space.

In 1924 the number of *passenger tickets* issued on the Great Western Railway reached 140,241,113, of which 107,168,577 were third-class and 31,612,071 workmen's. The total, which does not include season tickets, allows four journeys during the year for every inhabitant of England and Wales.

Coming to *goods traffic*, the total tonnage hauled was 81,723,133, which is thirteen times that of the Great Pyramid of Cheops. General merchandise accounted for 14,034,916 tons; coal, coke and patent fuel for 54,586,438 tons; and other minerals for the balance of 13,001,779 tons. Among general merchandise the following take the chief places, in round thousands of tons:— iron and steel, 4,263,000; stone, 2,268,000; timber, 1,958,000; grain, 816,000; bricks, 720,000; flour, 636,000.

A vast number of *live stock* travelled over the railway in the twelve months:—2,674,238 animals in all, including 1,345,843 sheep, 635,196 pigs, and 542,939 cattle.

While moving their loads passenger trains travelled 38,122,614 miles and goods trains 25,395,522 miles. Had one engine done all the work, shunting included, it would have run a distance equal to 4,000 circuits of the globe.

Now, traffic means wear and tear. So, in view of the preceding figures, we are not surprised to learn that

33,660 tons of new rails were laid during the year, 808,616 sleepers replaced, and 368,874 cubic yards of fresh ballast used to pack them. Fifty-two new locomotives were put into service, while 1,437 underwent heavy, and 533 light repairs in the railway workshops. For carriages the respective figures are 192, 3,961 and 15,384; and for wagons, 1,686, 17,432 and 176,138. These figures are a sufficient explanation of the huge works at Swindon.

To raise steam in the locomotives, coal worth £2,556,054 had to be shovelled into the fireboxes, and water to the value of £140,360 delivered to their boilers : while to keep them in running order about £60,000 was spent on lubricants, and £100,000 on other stores. On the traffic side, fuel, lighting, water, and general stores account for £283,000 ; wagon covers for £92,000* ; and cleaning, lubrication, and lighting of vehicles for £365,000.

From being 1,101 in 1851 the *Staff* of the Great Western Railway has grown into a huge army of over 117,000 persons, including 3,500 women. This army may be classified as follows :—

76 Capstanmen.

3,281 Carters and Vanguards.

1,242 Carriage Cleaners.

839 Carriage and Wagon Examiners.

384 Ditto, ditto, Oilers and Greasers.

1,638 Checkers.

18 Cranemen.

314 Crossing Keepers.

1,928 Engine Cleaners.

*In 1920 this item stood at £234,000. Other "odds and ends" of the same year were : £46,000 for cotton waste ; £6,000 for shunting poles : £11,000 for brooms and brushes ; £10,700 for ropes.

H

6,120 Engine Drivers and Motormen.

6,114 Firemen.

1,114 Foremen and Chargemen (non-supervisory).

3,274 Guards, goods.

1,111 Ditto, passenger.

5,864 Labourers.

340 Lampmen.

844 Loaders, Callers-off, Ropers, and Sheeters.

367 Messengers.

282 Number-takers.

12,350 Officers and Clerks.

10,888 Permanent Way Men.

26 Pointsmen.

378 Policemen.

37 Police Inspectors.

3,234 Porters, goods.

4,607 Ditto,   passenger.

630 Shop and Artisan Staff (supervisory grades).

21,820 Shop and Artisan Staff (excluding labourers and watchmen).

3,770 Shunters

1,580 Signal and Telegraph Men.

4,954 Signalmen.

1,294 Stationmasters and Yardmasters.

1,948 Supervisory Staff (other than shop and artisan and police staff).

721 Ticket Collectors.

100 Watchmen.

13,626 Miscellaneous.

On December 31, 1924, the *issued Capital* of the Great Western Railway stood at £146,442,493. The railway *receipts* for the year were £36,408,336 and *expenses* £30,339,505. Passenger traffic produced £10,844,047, and goods traffic £17,571,537. When compared with the " takings " in the early days of the Great Western, these figures show a complete reversal in the relative importance of the two kinds of traffic.

The growth of the Great Western Railway is demonstrated in a manner altogether different from a comparison of statistics when the first *Time Table* issued is contrasted with the latest edition available at the time of writing. On the one hand we have the single page of 1839, giving the times of trains running between Paddington and Maidenhead or West Drayton :—13 " down " and 14 " up " on on weekdays, and 8 " down " and 8 " up " on Sundays. On the other, a bulky volume of 260 large pages, 228 of which are solid time schedules, requiring an index in which the names of some 1,440 Great Western Railway stations appear, in addition to many of other Groups.

The item in the time tables that would probably most astonish the original Directorate of the Great Western Railway is that headed, " Through Express, Aberdeen to Penzance." This service, inaugurated in 1921, enables a passenger to travel the 785 miles from the Scottish port to Penzance in 21 hours, 50 minutes, or in the opposite direction in 20½ hours, *without changing carriages*, at an average speed of 36 to 38 miles an hour. This longest of non-change journeys in the United Kingdom was made possible by the co-operation of the Great Western and the London and North Eastern groups.

SOME DATES IN GREAT WESTERN RAILWAY HISTORY

1833, July	30—Public meeting held at Bristol to promote a railway from Bristol to London.
Aug.	19—First Meeting of Board of Management of the Company. Title of " Great Western Railway " recorded for the first time.
1833,	—First Prospectus of G.W.R. issued.
1835, Aug.	31—Great Western Railway Act received Royal Assent.
1838, June	4—G.W.R. opened from Paddington to Maidenhead Bridge.
1839,	—Electric Telegraph installed on line from Paddington to West Drayton.
1840, Mar.	30—G.W.R. extended to Reading.
June	1— ,, ,, Steventon.
July	20— ,, ,, Faringdon Road
Aug.	31— ,, ,, opened from Bristol to Bath.
Dec.	16— ,, extended to Wootton Bassett.
Dec.	16—First portion of Taff Vale Railway opened.
1841, May	31—G.W.R. extended to Chippenham.
June	30— ,, ,, Bath.
Aug.	31— ,, opened throughout to Bristol.
June	14—First portion of Bristol & Exeter Railway opened. Didcot to Oxford Branch opened.
1842, June	13—Queen Victoria made her first railway journey, on G.W.R.
Sept.	29—First excursion train from Bristol to London.
1843,	—Swindon-Gloucester line amalgamated with G.W.R.
1844.	—Didcot-Oxford branch amalgamated with G.W.R.
1846,	—Exeter-Newton Abbot section of S. Devon Railway opened. Cloak rooms for passengers' luggage inaugurated. Cardboard tickets adopted by G.W.R.
1847,	—Gloucester-Cheltenham Railway opened. Reading-Hungerford branch opened. Atmospheric system came into operation on S. Devon Railway.
1848,	—Shrewsbury and Chester Railway opened. S. Devon Railway opened to Plymouth and Torquay.

1849, OCT.	8	Windsor branch opened.
1850,		Chepstow-Swansea section of S. Wales Railway opened.
1851, JULY	1	Kennet and Avon Canal purchased by G.W.R.
		Chepstow-Grange Court section of S. Wales Railway opened.
1852,		West Cornwall Railway opened.
JULY	14	Chepstow Bridge completed. Route from London to S. Wales opened.
		Oxford-Birmingham line opened.
1853,		Hereford and Ludlow line opened.
1854, JAN.	17	New Station at Paddington opened.
		Maidenhead-High Wycombe branch opened.
		Shrewsbury and Chester, and Shrewsbury and Birmingham Railways amalgamated with G.W.R.
1856,		S. Wales Railway extended to New Milford.
1857,		Henley branch opened.
		Channel Islands steamboat service from Weymouth began.
1859, MAY	2	Saltash Bridge opened.
		Cornwall Railway opened.
SEPT.	15	Isambard Kingdom Brunel died.
1860,		First broad-gauge train ran from Paddington to Penzance.
		First interlocked signal frame used on G.W.R.
1862,		"Flying Dutchman" put on.
1863, JAN.	10	Metropolitan Railway opened, and worked by G.W.R.
AUG.	1	West Midland and S. Wales Railways amalgamated with G.W.R.
AUG.	24	Falmouth branch of Cornwall Railway opened.
		Spagnoletti block signal instruments introduced.
1864,		Mr. D. Gooch resigned post of Locomotive Superintendent.
		Hammersmith and City Railway opened.
1865,		Shrewsbury and Welshpool Railway amalgamated with G.W.R. and L. & N.W.R. jointly.
		Sir D. Gooch elected Chairman of G.W.R.
1869,		Broad gauge removed from Metropolitan Railway.
		Hereford, Ross and Gloucester Railway converted to narrow gauge.
1871,		"Caution" position of signals discontinued on G.W.R.
1872,		Severn Tunnel Act passed.
		South Wales Railway converted to narrow gauge.
1873,		Shah of Persia received at Paddington.

SOME DATES—*continued*.

1874,   —Quadrupling of G.W.R. tracks from London-Didcot begun.

1875,   —Vacuum brake adopted by G.W.R.

1876,   —West Cornwall and Bristol & Exeter Railways amalgamated with G.W.R.

1877,   —Bala and Dolgelley Railway amalgamated with G.W.R.

1878,   —South Devon Railway amalgamated with G.W.R.
Subway for Hammersmith and City Railway between Paddington and Westbourne Park opened.

1879,   —Severn Bridge opened.
Iron wagon frames introduced on G.W.R.

1880,   —Paddington Station lighted by electricity.

1881,   —Headings of Severn Tunnel met.

1882,   —Third-class on all G.W.R. passenger trains except certain expresses.

1886, JAN. 9—First goods train ran through Severn Tunnel.

     DEC. 1—First passenger train ran through Severn Tunnel.

1888,   —" Great Western Railway Magazine " started.

1890,   —First corridor train on G.W.R.

     OCT. 1—Third-class on all G.W.R. passenger trains.

1893,   —Steam heating of trains introduced on G.W.R.

1895,   —Compulsory ten minute stop at Swindon abolished.
Water-troughs laid on G.W.R. tracks.
Bath and Bristol services accelerated.

1896,   —First-class dining-cars started.
Paddington Station Hotel reverted to G.W.R. control.

     OCT. 13—Fast service to Devon and Cornwall announced.

1899,   —Non-stop London-Exeter and London-Birmingham trains put on.

1901, JULY 1—Stert-Westbury " cut-off " opened.
Third-class saloons introduced.
Chain communication inside carriages adopted.

1903, JULY 1—South Wales Direct route opened for passenger trains.

     AUG. 3—First G.W.R. motor-bus put into service.
Rail motor-cars introduced.
Third-class dining-cars on expresses.

1904, JULY 1—London-Plymouth non-stop express put on.

1905,   —Incandescent gas lighting of carriages introduced.
First power signalling equipment installed (Didcot).

1906, JAN. 1—Audible signalling on locomotives tried.

SOME DATES—*continued.*

1906, JUNE 29—Castle Cary-Langport " cut-off " opened.

JULY —" Cornish Riviera Express " inaugurated.

AUG. 30—Fishguard-Rosslare service began.

1908, —" Pacific " locomotive, " Great Bear," put into service.

1910, —Ashenden-Aynho " cut-off," and short route to Birmingham opened.

OCT. 1—Second-class abolished on G.W.R.

1914, AUG. 4—G.W.R. taken over by Government.

1915, FEB. 1—G.W.R. district raided by Zeppelins.

1920, AUG. 3—Ealing and Shepherd's Bush Railway opened.

1921, AUG. 15—Government control ceased.

OCT. 3—Through service between Aberdeen and Penzance inaugurated.

1923, JAN. 1—Great Western Group began to function.

JULY 9—Cheltenham-Paddington express booked to run 61.8 m.p.h. between Swindon and Paddington.

1924 —Introduction on G.W.R. of 20-ton wagons.

INDEX

INDEX—*continued.*

INDEX—*continued.*

INDEX—*continued.*

INDEX—*continued.*